HICKMANS

P9-DNB-334

simply
**felt**

WITHDRAWN

Brunswick County Library
100 W. Moore Street
Southport NC 28461

# simply felt

## 20 easy and elegant designs in wool

**MARGARET DOCHERTY**

**JAYNE EMERSON**

INTERWEAVE PRESS
www.interweave.com

Design and Production: Anne Wilson
Technical Editors: Sharon Costello, Amy Clarke Moore
Production: Samantha L. Thaler, Dean Howes
Photographer: John Heseltine
Proofreader and indexer: Marie Lorimer

Created, designed, and edited by:
Berry & Co.
47 Crewys Road
Child's Hill, London, NW2 2AU, U.K.

Text and designs copyright © 2004 Margaret Docherty and Jayne Emerson
Illustration copyright © 2004 Carol Hill
Photography copyright © 2004 John Heseltine

All rights reserved.

**INTERWEAVE PRESS**
201 East Fourth Street
Loveland, Colorado 80537-5655 USA
www.interweave.com

Printed in Singapore by Tien Wah Press (Pte) Limited

Library of Congress Cataloging-in-Publication Data
Docherty, Margaret.
  Simply felt : 20 easy and elegant designs in wool / Margaret Docherty
  & Jayne Emerson.
     p. cm.
  Includes bibliographical references and index.
  ISBN 1-931499-70-5
  1. Felt work. I. Emerson, Jayne. II. Title.
  TT880.D59 2004
  746'.0463--dc22

                      2004006408

10 9 8 7 6 5 4 3 2 1

# contents

Introduction     6

**Machine-washed fulled fabric**     12
Pot holder     16
Hot-water bottle cover     20
Flower pillow     24
Patchwork pillow     28

**Flat felt**     32
Book covers     38
Shoulder bag     42
Simple briefcase     46

**Decorative flat felt**     50
Zigzag muffler     54
Chiffon scarf     58
Table runner     62
Silk inlaid lampshade     66
Patchwork runner     70
Bucket bag     74

**Seamless felt**     78
Slippers     82
Spotted slippers     86
Children's slippers     87
Inlaid containers     88
Tea cozy     92
Holdall bag     96
Cloche hat     98
Pillbox hat     102
Small purse     104
Glasses case     108
Child's silk-lined jacket     110
Pictorial pillow     114

**Useful information**     118
Preparing fleeces     119
Dyeing wool     120
Stitching     122
Felt flowers     123
Templates     124
Care of felt     126
Suppliers     127
Acknowledgments     127
Index     128

# introduction

As one of us is a traditional felt maker and the other is a textile designer, we believed it was appropriate to join forces to create a gallery of projects with contemporary appeal, in the hope of encouraging a new generation to take up a wonderfully versatile and rewarding craft.

The felted projects in this book are principally created with traditional hand felt making techniques, but we have also included a few "quick" felted projects in which pure wool fabric is put through a hot wash cycle in the machine to make a felt fabric. The latter method lacks the refinement or the quality of true felt making or the necessary control for carefully sized garments, but can be fun to use for household objects, such as patchwork pillows or pot holders. One of the virtues of machine-wash felting is that it recycles worn or outgrown garments. You may, too, have accidentally felted a favorite sweater at one time or another and wondered what to do with it.

The projects in the book range from very simple household items to more beautifully worked, true felt projects. Whatever you make, it will only be as good as the original wool from which it was created. It is important to discover as much as you can about the nature and properties of wool, because, as with

any craft, the better you understand the medium, the more control you are going to have over the finished item.

Because hand-making felt is such a tactile experience, no piece of felt is ever quite like another. Felters create their own version of felt, as knitters all knit to different tensions. The great joy of felt making is that it is truly natural and simple; it relies on natural fibers, soap, and water, and some hard work to produce the textile. The process is fun (particularly if you work in a group) and a great stress-buster; all that rubbing and pummeling is ideal for working off the tensions of everyday living, and, marvelously, you have something permanent, practical, and beautiful to show for it!

Felt is a wonderfully versatile textile. It can be used to make many different kinds of objects, both two-dimensional and three-dimensional. In the felt making process, natural wool fibers are soaked with hot water and rubbed together to create a dense, non-fraying, and remarkably durable fabric. The fact that felt is flexible but does not fray has led to its use in many different industries, from the green baize on card and pool tables to piano hammer covers, as well as its more widely known uses in the fashion industry for such things as hats, slippers, and socks.

### history of felt

It is thought felt was first made in the Bronze Age, well before wool fibers were spun and woven. Felt

hangings, socks and stockings, cushion rugs and carpets, saddle covers and blankets dating back to 600–200 B.C. have been found in Siberian tombs, preserved by the frozen temperatures of the area. Even as early as this, felt was used decoratively as well as functionally; the Altai people of Siberia considered felt an art as much as a craft. Similar finds have been unearthed in Mongolia—where tribesmen today live in felt huts known as yurts—and in China, Korea and Japan, where it is still a thriving industry.

As with many textiles, felt making is often a group activity in nomadic communities. While the processes of making the felt are broadly the same—soaking with hot water, rubbing with soap, and then pummeling the fibers to mat them together—the practice varies. We tend to roll our felts up in a rattan blind or mat and push this backward and forward to harden it. In Mongolia, when making large yurt panels or rugs, a similar reed mat is used but this is dragged behind horses over the Steppes for several hours!

Felt hats are traditional in many countries, from the earliest caps worn by the Phrygians to the smart fedoras still made using traditional felting methods in parts of the Piedmont in Italy today.

### all about wool

All kinds of natural animal fiber can be used to make felt. Many felt makers prefer to use Merino wool, because it shrinks readily, thereby speeding up the felting process. Different kinds of wool felt better than others, and generally wools that have a natural luster and a fine crimp (those which do not spring back into shape when squeezed) are the best. First-time felters should use Merino wool top, which felts easily.

Although you could buy wool direct from the sheep rancher as raw fleeces, most felt makers are more likely to buy their wool fleeces already carded and scoured.

Each wool fiber is covered with a protective membrane with scales that point toward the tip of the fiber. The scales are designed to move dirt and moisture away from the sheep's body. They are also designed to keep the sheep cool in the summer and warm in the winter by opening up or closing down.

Felting takes advantage of these properties—when heat and moisture are applied the scales open up. Agitating the fibers moves them closer together, and submerging the fibers in cold water causes the scales to close and lock down. The result is a permanently interlocked matt of fibers—a felted fabric.

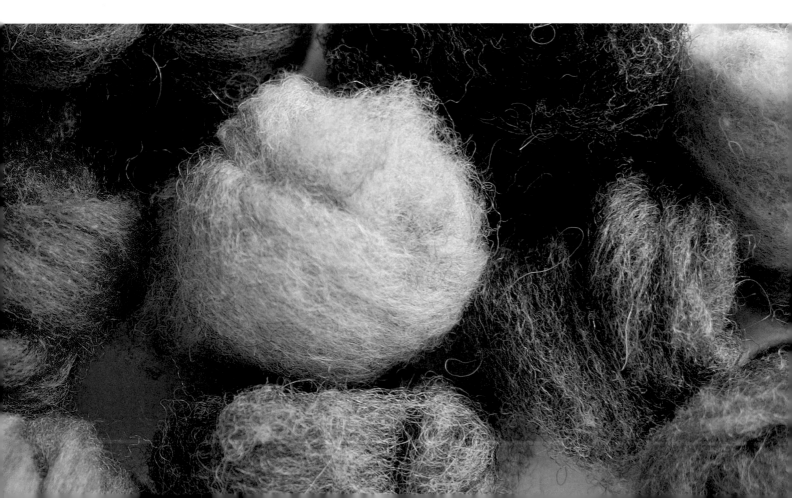

### why use soap?

Felting creates a fabric from a mass of wool fibers that previously had no structure through the process of agitation, hot water, and soap.

Wool has a natural pH factor (determining its level of acidity or alkalinity) of around 3 to 7, which is in the neutral range. To encourage wool to felt more rapidly acidity or alkalinity needs to be encouraged; either will do (although too much alkalinity will permanently damage wool fibers—they will become weak and brittle).

In primitive communities, vinegar or urine, both being acid, were used for felt making. In our more hygiene-conscious era, we prefer to use soap, which has a high alkaline factor. Different felt makers prefer different kinds of soap, but olive oil soap is highly regarded as it is smooth to work with and less hard on your hands. You can also use Dawn dishwashing detergent—it's pH neutral and safe for wool and human hands. (In fact, it pays to use good quality hand cream on your hands regularly when felt making as the combination of

frequent immersion in water and the rubbing can cause dry, chafed skin.) Some felt makers prefer to use rubber gloves for this reason.

### felt forms

Felt can be immensely thick or paper thin. The thickness is made up from several layers of fiber laid on top of each other, each layer at right angles or perpendicular to the previous one. The quality of hardness is determined by how much the fibers are shrunk in the process, and this is done in two ways:

first by rubbing the fibers together with warm, soapy water and then by rolling the partially felted fabric backward and forward in a mat or around a stick, usually with further hand work, to create a really dense, durable textile.

A growing range of artists and textile designers have become interested in the versatile properties of felt. Since the late 1960s, textile artists in Europe and North America have been exploring all aspects of fiber art; some use felt to create a wonderfully diverse range of artifacts, from felted chairs to stunning designer dresses.

# machine-washed fulled fabric

The projects in this chapter are all made from pure wool knitted or crocheted textiles that have been washed at high temperatures; this simple technique makes a good introduction to felting for those new to the craft. The fulling process happens automatically in the washing machine where the combination of hot water, agitation, and soap quickly mats the wool fibers into a dense fabric, shrinking it considerably from its original size (as many of us have already experienced, having inadvertently "fulled" a favorite sweater in the washing machine). The resulting felted textile does not fray and can be cut and stitched to create useful household accessories—pillow covers, pot holders, hot-water bottle covers and the like.

# FULLING FABRIC IN THE WASHING MACHINE

Transforming an ordinary knitted or woven wool fabric into a fulled fabric is very easy—especially if you have a washing machine handy. The thicker the knitting, and the more fulled it is, the better its insulating properties will be. However, the machine-washing process is far from exact so it is not a suitable technique for items that demand careful measurement. It does work well for projects such as pillow covers, hot-water bottle covers and pot holders, for example. If the knitting has a patterned stitch, the resulting fulled textile will also be interestingly textured. You can also incorporate small patches of knitting into the handmade felt process (see the tea cozy on pages 92–95).

The amount of shrinkage on any piece of knitting varies greatly, so you need to practice first with some old pieces to check the appropriate temperatures. Normally this will be in the range of 140–194 degrees F (60–90 degrees C). Remember that only pure wool will full—wool substitutes won't, so you have to check the labels first. Be warned, too, that some finishing agents used by manufacturers can impede the fulling process.

**MATERIALS**

PIECE OF SUITABLE KNITTING (SWEATER OR SCARF) OF PURE WOOL

WASHING MACHINE

WOOL-SAFE SOAP SUCH AS EUCALAN OR DAWN DISHWASHING SOAP

SCISSORS

TAPE MEASURE

# preparing to full

**1** Check the fiber content on the washing instruction label. Only pure wool (marked with a symbol) is suitable, including mixed wool fibers, such as mohair, angora or cashmere. "Washable" wools will not felt.

**2** Measure the piece (A).

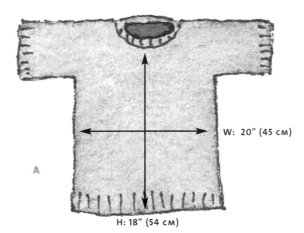

W: 20" (45 см)

H: 18" (54 см)

A

# the fulling process

**1** Wash the piece on a hot wash (a 140 degree F /60 degree C with two tablespoons of soap) cycle and then measure the piece to check the degree of shrinkage (B). If it fulled down well, it is now ready for use. If not, put it through the machine on a similar setting and check again.

**2** Ensure the piece is well rinsed; hang it out to dry. You should now be able to cut the knitting without it fraying at the edges.

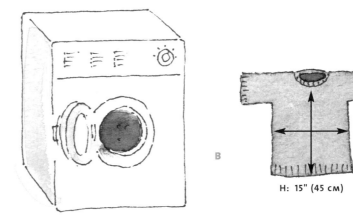

W: 12" (30 см)

H: 15" (45 см)

B

### FELTED SAMPLES

The two samples shown here demonstrate the effects of machine washing wool. A relatively open weave quickly becomes a matted, hard fabric, which can be cut without fraying. The degree of shrinkage depends on the program used. Tumble dryers will further felt wool, even in a relatively short time.

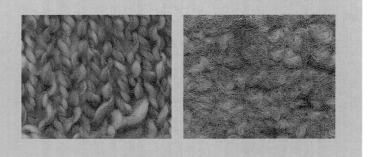

# pot holder

This is one of the easiest projects to make. Felt is ideal for this purpose, as you need a fabric that offers plenty of insulation. For the project shown here, we used a chunky knit scarf bought from a thrift shop, and popped it into the washing machine on the hottest water setting. It created a beautifully fulled effect, and shrank the fabric down by about half.

This pot holder is made with an opening so you can put your hand inside, and use it like an oven mitt. If you line the holder with quilt batting, you will create an even more effective heat barrier.

**MATERIALS**

PIECE OF TEXTURED
    KNITTING

SMALL PIECE OF WHITE FELT
    AND A SCRAP OF RED FELT

NEEDLE AND THREAD

CARDBOARD AND SCISSORS

DIAGONAL SET TRIANGLE RULER

LINING MATERIAL

# HOW TO MAKE IT

This is very much a beginner's project, made from a piece of knitting that was washed using very hot water (see page 15). This particular piece of felt was formerly a chunky knit scarf, but you could full any suitable knitted or crocheted textile. Remember that thinner pieces will need to be given a thick lining to make them more heatproof. Because the pot holder is small, you can stitch it by hand. If you want to decorate the front, do so before stitching the pieces of the pot holder together.

## creating the design

A

**1** It is best to full the knitted garment in its entirety first, following the instructions on pages 14–15. If you cut the piece of knitting beforehand, it is likely to fray during washing. Allow to dry.

**2** Mark out a square to the desired size, using a diagonal set triangle ruler to ensure the sides are at right angles to each other (**A**). The pot holder here measures 9" (23 cm) square.

**3** Using sharp scissors, cut out two identical pieces for the back and front of the pot holder (decorate the front of the pot holder at this point).

**4** Cut out two more pieces of felt to the same size as the outer layers to provide a lining for the pot holder.

# adding the flower

**1** To decorate the front of the pot holder, draw a five-petaled flower on a piece of cardboard and cut it out.

**2** Lay the template on the white felt and cut out the flower. Cut out a small bright red or orange circle for the center.

**3** Position the flower, with the cut out circle on top, in the center of the holder. Stitch through both layers, using a stab stitch (see page 122), (**B**).

**B**

# finishing off

**1** Sandwich the lining between the two pieces of the pot holder, wrong sides facing, and pin and baste in position (**c**).

**2** Backstitch (see page 122) around three sides, ½" (1 cm) in from the edge.

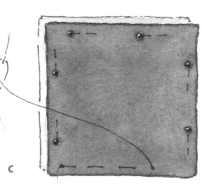

**C**

**3** To add a loop to the pot holder, cut out a narrow strip of machine-made felt or use a scrap from another handmade felt project. Double it to make a loop (**D**) measuring about 3" (8 cm) long and overcast the ends to the upper corner (opposite any opening) of the pot holder.

**D**

**ALTERNATIVE MOTIF**
If you wish, make a little star for the front of the pot holder from a piece of surplus felt. A little heart-shaped button has been used to attach it to the pot holder.

# hot-water bottle cover

Hot-water bottle covers are becoming surprisingly popular, particularly when you need a little pampering. This simple hot-water bottle cover is made from fabric fulled in the washer. The fabric has great insulating properties and is wonderfully soft and warm. It makes good use of a favorite sweater or cardigan, either when it has become worn or if it has already been shrunk by mistake. This particular cover has been made from a stockinette-stitch sweater, and the plain stitch is the ideal surface for embellishment.

The motif chosen is a simple outlined flower, but you could design your own.

**MATERIALS**

**KNITTED GARMENT WITH RIB**
**(AT LEAST 50 PERCENT**
**LARGER THAN THE SIZE OF**
**THE BOTTLE TO ALLOW**
**FOR SHRINKAGE)**

**TAPE MEASURE OR RULER**

**NEEEDLE AND THREAD**

**COTTON BATTING (3"[8 CM]**
**LARGER THAN THE SIZE OF**
**THE BOTTLE)**

**ALTERNATIVE MOTIF**
You can use any motif for the
front that you like. A little stab-
stitched heart is another fun
choice.

# HOW TO MAKE IT

A hot-water bottle is the perfect project to reclaim a worn out or accidentally fulled sweater. Either use a discarded one of your own or hunt out an appropriate piece of knitting or crochet in the local thrift shop.

The design shown here is very easy to make, but you need to measure your own hot-water bottle first, to ensure the cover fits. If you want to add a front pocket (for warming your hands) just add a square of felted fabric to the front, decorate it with any motif, and stab stitch (see page 122) the pocket in place along the top and bottom edges.

## making the template

**1** Make the fabric using the machine-washed fulling method (see pages 14–15), and allow to dry.

**2** Trace around the hot-water bottle that you intend to cover (the sizes often vary so it is best to make your own template), making sure you leave a 1" (2.5 cm) allowance all around to allow for ease of fit and for seam allowances (**A**).

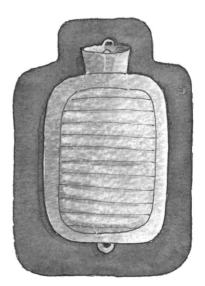

A

# making the cover

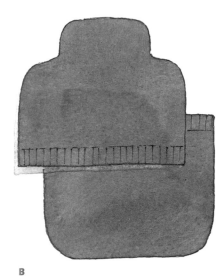

B

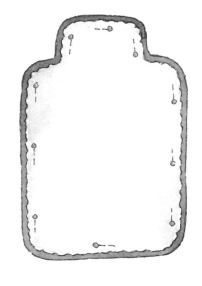

C

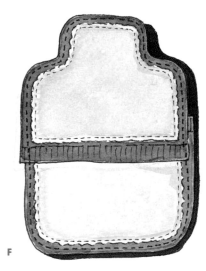

D

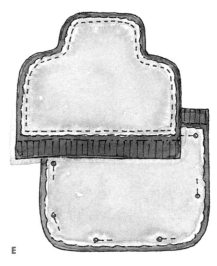

E

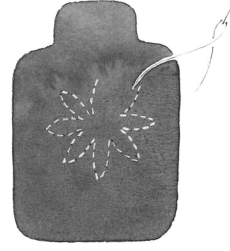

F

**1** Cut out a front piece from the fulled knitting to the required size, and cut two pieces for the back (**B**), positioning them so that the rib of the sweater forms each back opening, and the back pieces overlap each other, as shown, by 2½" (6 cm).

**2** Cut a front piece the same size as the felt top from the cotton batting (**C**), and cut two back pieces just ½" (1 cm) shorter than the top back pieces, so the batting will not be visible when all the pieces are stitched together. Then apply the front piece of batting to the wrong side of the front fulled piece. Pin together.

**3** Hand quilt the design on the front using stab stitches (**D**).

**4** Apply the back pieces of batting to the back pieces of the hot-water bottle cover, again on the wrong side, and machine stitch together (**E**).

**5** Stitch the front and two overlapped back pieces wrong sides together by hand or machine (**F**). Turn right side out.

# flower pillow

A man's sweater is perfect for this project, especially as the muted colors often used in menswear, such as gray, olive green, or navy, look smart in this contemporary design. They are quick and easy to make, so you can make several pillows in one evening, once you have fulled the knitting for the fabric. However, do not wash colored fabrics together—they might run! While one pillow can sport an appliqué detail as shown, the others could rely on the texture of the original sweater (for example, a cabled knit) for a more graphic effect.

**MATERIALS**

LARGE KNITTED WOOL
    GARMENT WITH RIB (AT
    LEAST 30 BY 30" [75 BY
    75 CM]) WITH ENOUGH
    SURPLUS TO MAKE 3
    FLOWERS

NEEDLE AND THREAD

SMALL CRYSTAL BEADS

PILLOW FORM, 16" (40 CM)
    SQUARE

# HOW TO MAKE IT

This simply decorated pillow is made with an envelope opening at the back, into which the pillow form is inserted. For the pillow, you will need a piece of fulled fabric large enough to cut a 17" (42 cm) square for the front, and two smaller pieces measuring 17 by 10" (42 by 25 cm) each for the back. If you use a large sweater for the felt, you can use the ribbed areas to make a neat finish to the back opening on the pillow. In this design, three flowers are grouped in one corner, but you could scatter them over the surface of the pillow, or center them on the pillow front.

## creating the design

**1** Machine wash the knitted garment or textile on a 140 degree F (60 degree C) setting. Check that the fabric has fulled and, if necessary, wash again to shrink down further.

**2** Cut out the main piece for the front of the pillow, measuring 17" (42 cm) square (**A**).

**3** Then cut the two pieces for the back, which should overlap by a couple of inches (**B**). Use the rib of the sweater, if possible, for the edges of the back opening to create an attractive finish.

A

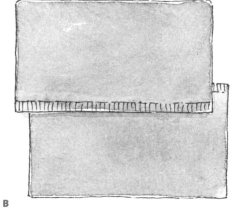

B

**3** Create the three felt flowers by copying the design (**C**) for a five-petaled flower below. Cut out six flowers, two for each flower decoration, from the sleeves of the sweater (or the surplus fabric).

**4** Make each pair of flowers, with the top flower at a different angle from the one beneath, and stitch the flowers to one corner of the pillow, using a few crystal beads in the center of each to anchor them in position (**D**).

**5** Finally, put the pillow pieces right sides together as shown (**E**), and machine stitch around the edges, leaving a ½" (1 cm) seam allowance. Turn the pillow cover right side out, and insert the pillow form.

C

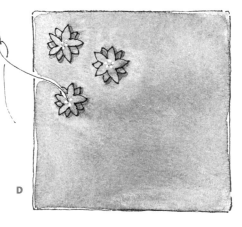

D

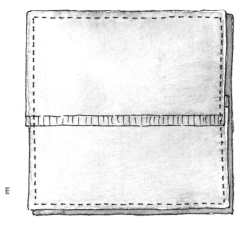

E

### ALTERNATIVE MOTIFS

You can make a variety of motifs, including the little double-star pattern or a double-petaled flower with a contrasting center. If you wish, use a decorative button to stitch the motif to the pillow.

# patchwork pillow

Patchwork makes wonderful use of scraps of fulled wool fabric; what better way than to make a pillow or child's blanket from cast-off, shrunk or outgrown sweaters, or equally small leftovers from other felt projects you have made? This patchwork pillow has been made using fabric fulled in the washer—which is still pleasantly soft—and employs a sophisticated palette of neutral and pastel colors. Because the felted knitting does not fray, you can turn the exposed seams into a design element.

If you wish, you can decorate individual squares with embroidered motifs or stitch them in contrasting wool. The patches can be put together in a random design or organized in particular patterns.

## MATERIALS

MACHINE-FULLED FELT
IN FOUR COLORS PLUS
ENOUGH WITH A RIBBED
EDGE TO MAKE TWO
PIECES 19 BY 12" (47 BY
30 CM) FOR THE BACK

NEEDLE AND THREAD

18" (45 CM) SQUARE PILLOW
FORM

# HOW TO MAKE IT

This simple patchwork design is for a pillow measuring 18" (45 cm) square. It is made from 18 patches, each measuring 6 by 3" (15 by 8 cm), plus seam allowance, with an envelope opening at the back into which the pillow form can be inserted. The patched pieces of fulled wool are pieced together in three strips, which are then stab-stitched together (see page 123), with the seams exposed as a decorative feature (since the fulled fabric does not fray when cut). Four colorways were used for this design, but you can adapt this as you wish, depending on the pieces of knitting that you have available. A simpler alternative would be to piece together four squares of fulled fabric (using 9½" [25 cm] squares for an 18" [45 cm] square pillow) and stitch them together with bright wool yarn.

## creating the design

1 Make a paper template to the size of each patch (A). Plan the positions of the chosen colors (B).

2 Using the template, cut out 18 rectangles of machine-washed fulled fabric in the chosen colors.

6½" (16 CM)

3½"
(10 CM)

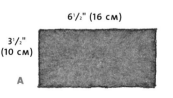

A

B

# stitching the patches (either by hand or machine)

**1** Stitch the patches, wrong sides together, along the long sides. Sewing the patches wrong sides together creates a visible seam on the right side. Sew six patches in this way to form one long row (c).

**2** Make up the other two rows in the same way.

**3** Stitch the rows together, wrong sides facing, continuing to create a visible seam on the right side (D). Joining all three rows forms a square.

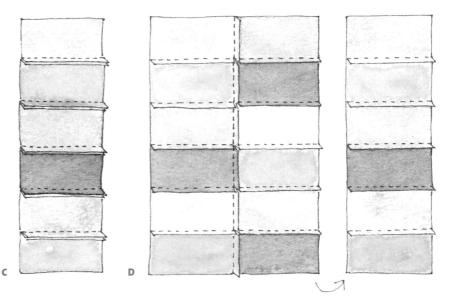

# making the pillow

**1** Cut out the two pieces of machine-fulled fabric for the back, each measuring 19 by 21" (47 by 53 cm) to create an envelope opening at the back of the pillow.

**2** With the right sides facing, join the two backing pieces to the right front as shown, and stitch around the sides using stab stitch (E), or machine sew.

**3** Insert the pillow form through the opening.

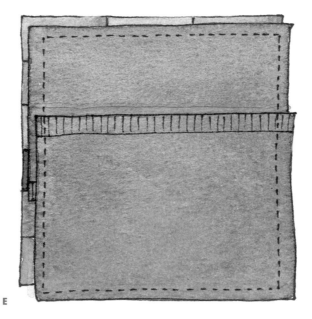

# flat felt

The projects in this section are all made from simple flat felt. The thickness and hardness of the felt varies according to its purpose and function. For durability, three or four layers of thick felt are needed, but for decorative purposes a couple of thin layers will be just fine.

If you wish, you can create the layers in different colors. This is particularly useful when making any kind of container, such as a bag, for example, where you might want to expose the lining. For three-layered felt, you could make the first layer for the lining in one color, and the top layer or layers in a second color.

The container shapes in this section are all stitched together. For shapes made in the round, without stitching, see Seamless Felt on pages 78–117.

# MAKING FELT

Felting is a process of permanently interlocking wool fibers into a dense fabric using water, agitation, and soap. It is rooted in the oldest traditions of textile making, and practiced by many different cultures all over the world.

The great joy of felt making is that it needs no special equipment or even a proper workshop. You can make it all on the kitchen table, but you will need a supply of water and the means to heat it up close by.

If you do use your kitchen table, be prepared! You will need to cover the table with a waterproof cover, as quite a lot of water gets sloshed around in the process. You can lay a towel out on top of the cover to mop up any surplus water and a rattan blind or mat on top of the towel—then you're ready to begin making felt.

## preparation for flat felt

Gather together a sufficient quantity of wool top for the size and weight of felt required and organize your workspace as above.

When making felt, the aim is to create an even, dense, hard-wearing fabric. To do this, you tease out tufts from the wool top and lay them down in layers, trying to get the tufts as evenly spread as possible, so there are no holes and gaps. To this end, you lay one layer of tufts down in one direction, and the next perpendicular to it, which helps to ensure there are no unexpected holes, which would make the felt less durable and strong.

Make sure you have paper, pencil, and scissors nearby. You will also need a suitable place to dry the felt. You can hang a small piece over a chair back. A piece made from three or four layers of wool top will normally take about eight hours to dry.

**MATERIALS**

(FOR THREE-LAYERED PIECE OF FLAT FELT, 12" [30 CM] SQUARE):

ABOUT 2 OZ (60 G) OF MERINO WOOL TOP

NET CURTAIN

RATTAN BLIND

OLIVE OIL SOAP

WARM WATER

APRON AND RUBBER GLOVES (OPTIONAL)

# creating the layers

**1** Using the prepared work surface , take a section of the fleece from the wool top and, holding it a good 5" (12 cm) from the end, pull out a tuft about 5 in (12 cm) long (A) and smooth out the strands.

**2** Lay the first tuft down in one corner on the prepared surface and then lay subsequent tufts side by side in a row (about 12" [30 cm] long in this case). Then make another row of tufts next to it, facing the same direction, and so on (B), until you have created a 12" (30 cm) square. This creates the first layer of felt. To make the second layer, lay down the next layer of tufts perpendicular to the first layer. To make a third layer, lay the tufts down perpendicular to the previous layer. Check it for any holes or gaps and fill if necessary.

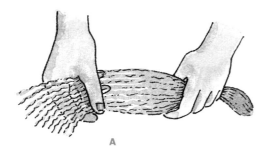

A

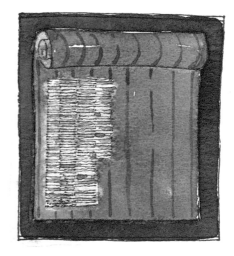

B

# the felting process

**1** You can now start to wet the wool fibers to begin the process of felting them together. Cover the layers with a net curtain. Then, using hand-hot, soapy water, wet the felt. Make sure you wet the entire area thoroughly but not to the point of it being awash. However, the wool should be distinctly wet, rather than simply damp. Press flat.

**2** Taking the bar of soap, gently rub the surface of the net with it. Using the flats of your hands in a circular motion, exert just enough pressure to rub the fibers together without shifting the wool tufts.

**3** Once you have flattened and meshed the fibers (it takes about 15 minutes of rubbing), you can then turn the piece over and repeat Steps 1 and 2. If some areas are softer than others (right), continue rubbing until the felt is firm and even textured.

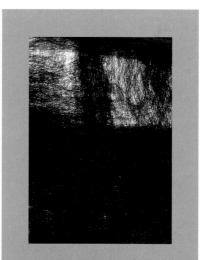

**A partially rubbed-in piece of felt. Further rubbing will create a more even texture.**

# fulling the felt

Once the tops have felted together to form a fabric that you can pick up in its entirety, you can begin the next stage of the process. This is known as "fulling" and during it the partially made felt is hardened and thickened into its final, highly durable fabric.

**1** Wet with hot water and roll the piece of felt in the blind or mat (**A**) and push it backward and forward with both hands (**B**). You may have to do this for about 10 minutes or so, occasionally changing direction, so that the fabric will shrink in both directions.

**2** Remove the felt from the mat. If it has now become obviously thickened and hardened, you can rinse it off first in hot water and then in cold to remove all the soap (**c**). If it is insufficiently hardened, repeat the rolling process for a few more minutes and then rinse off.

**3** Roll the felt in a towel to remove the excess water then lay on a dry towel or on a chair back (**D**) to dry.

A

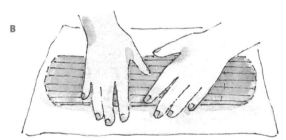

B

C

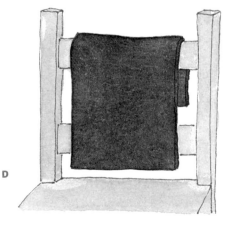

D

# felt thicknesses

Felt can be made in many different thicknesses. Individual felters produce thinner or thicker results depending on a) how thickly each lays down the strands of wool tops and b) how much time and effort each spends on the actual felting process. No two felters produce identical results, and it is precisely this individual quality that gives felt its charm.

As far as the thickness and the number of layers of felt to use for a specific project, much depends on the final purpose of the design. Most of the felt designs in this book are made using two or three layers of felt, although a rug, for example, could require five or six. You can, if you wish, make one layer of felt (the underside) a different color from the top side. If the felt is three-layered, simply use one color of wool top for one layer, and a second color for the other layers.

The pieces of felt demonstrate the variety of thicknesses. Some are two-, some three-layers thick, and some have more than one color.

**SPECIAL TIPS AND TECHNIQUES**

• Be patient! Make sure that you rub the entire area to be felted slowly and consistently, to produce a fabric of even thickness. Pay particular attention to the edges, as it is only too easy to produce a piece of felt that is dense in the center and almost paper-thin around the edges. Changing direction when rolling will help produce a more even texture.

• Check at intervals to see how well the fibers have felted together. The more you rub, the more the fibers will shrink down and interlock.

• Make sure you rinse all traces of soap from the felt and ensure the felt is properly dry before you put it away.

• If your skin becomes sensitive to the constant exposure to water and soap, use rubber gloves.

# book covers

Felt is an excellent choice for a book or album cover owing to the durability and toughness of the fabric. These notebook covers have been designed using a simple binding system in which elastic bands (see suppliers on page 127) have been threaded through the hole-punched pages of the notebook and the cover itself, although you could use a ribbon if you prefer. You can make the flat felt for the cover using just one color or create a contrasting reverse side using another color for the inside layer.

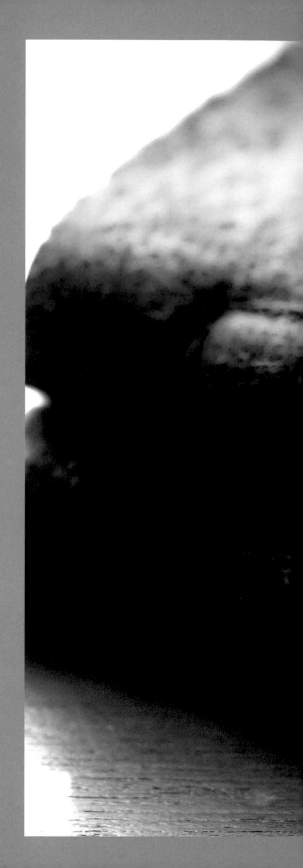

**MATERIALS**

½ oz (14 g) Merino wool top (outside) and ¼ oz (7 g) wool top (inside)

FELTING EQUIPMENT (SEE PAGE 34)

TAILOR'S CHALK

HOLE PUNCH

ELASTIC BANDS

RULER

# HOW TO MAKE IT

These book covers are made from three layers of felt created from wool top and measure 6 by 4" (15 by 10 cm). They are very simple to make but the felt needs to be both thick and strong, and well hardened. Remember to allow for the height, depth, and thickness of the pages,  and add an inch or so all around for shrinkage during felting. The instructions here are for a notebook cover with a contrasting color on the inside cover, created from the first layer of fiber that you put down. If you wish, you could add a decorative motif, or embroidery, to the front cover before binding it to the notebook pages.

## making the felt

**1** Prepare the work surface (see page 34). Decide on the size required, and remember to allow a little extra for shrinkage all around. If you wish, you can chalk the rough measurements on the work surface to act as a guide.

**2** Tease out wool top tufts about 5" (12 cm) long  of the first color and lay them down side by side in rows on the mat until you have covered the area.

**3** Taking the second color, proceed in the same way, but lay the tufts down perpendicular to the previous layer (**A**).

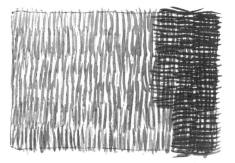

**A**

**4** Again using the second color, lay down a third layer perpendicular to the second layer.

**5** Cover the layers with the net and wet the felt (see page 35).

**6** Once the fibers are thoroughly interlocked, you can start the fulling process (see page 36). When the felt is sufficiently thickened and hardened, rinse the piece (see page 36) and hang it to dry.

# cutting out the cover

**1** You now need precise measurements, so measure out the depth and height of pages of the notebook, and the thickness. You will need to cut the felt to twice the measurements of the page width and depth (to allow for back and front covers), and the thickness (to allow for the spine width).

**2** Mark out the measurements with tailor's chalk on the felt (**B**), and cut out the felt to these measurements.

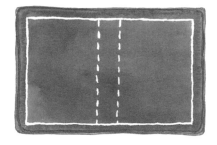

**B**

# creating the binding

**1** Mark the center line of the notebook pages. Using a hole punch, punch two holes on the left-hand side of the pages, ensuring all the pages are similarly punched (**c**).

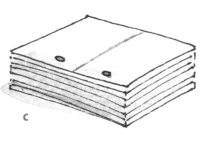

**C**

**D**

**2** Mark the points on the front and back covers that align with these holes, and create matching holes using a hole punch tool. Thread an elastic band through the back cover (**D**).

**3** Then thread the band through the pages, and finally through the front cover.

**E**

**CONTRASTING LINING**

The book cover shown here has two colors of felt. In this case, the yellow is used for the inside.

# shoulder bag

This simple shoulder bag is quite small. It measures 7" (18 cm) wide by 9" (23 cm) deep, but you could easily make it larger without in any way changing the design. It is made from two pieces of flat felt that are stab-stitched to a narrow gusset that runs between them, with a long piece of felt for the strap. Using contrasting colors for the button and loop fastening gives the bag an attractive finishing touch. Choosing a dark color (such as bottle green, navy or black, for example) makes a bag that can last for a long time and still look great!

**MATERIALS**

4 OZ (115 G) MERINO WOOL
    TOP FOR THE BAG

MERINO WOOL TOP IN
    THREE COLORS FOR
    FASTENING

FELTING EQUIPMENT (SEE
    PAGE 34)

NEEDLE AND YARN

RULER

TAILOR'S CHALK

SCISSORS

# HOW TO MAKE IT

The front, back, and gussets of the bag are made using three layers of plain felt (see pages 34–36). You can either cut the strap from the main felt for the bag or create a separate piece of felt using the table edge as a guide; this piece of felt is then doubled over and stitched. The buttons and loop are made from rolled pieces of felt made from contrasting layers of wool top (as in the book covers on pages 38–41). First create the layers of felt for the bag and strap, and then create the multicolored felt for the buttons and loop. If you want to make a seamless bag with a flap, adapt the instructions for the purse on pages 104–107, using the sizes and quantities of wool top suggested here.

## making the felt

**1** Using a prepared work surface , lay down the first layer of wool top (see page 35) and make two more layers, each perpendicular to the previous ones.

**2** Cover with net, wet the fibers, and press flat. Rub for about 10 minutes. Once the fibers have interlocked, roll the felt in a blind or mat, add very hot water, and roll backward and forward in both directions for several minutes until the felt has hardened. Rinse well and leave overnight to dry.

**3** When the felt is thoroughly dry, lay the felt on the table and cut out templates for the bag, enlarging those shown right (**A**) to your chosen size. Lay these on the felt, marking the shapes using tailor's chalk.

**4** Cut out the front and back of the bag, measure around the sides of one to establish the gusset length, and cut this as one long piece or two shorter ones (plus a seam allowance), which are then stitched together. Cut a strip of felt for the handle to the chosen length (**A**).

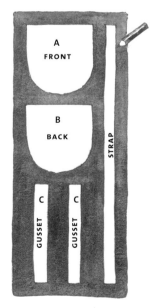

A

# making the bag

**1** Stitch the gusset (stitching the two pieces together first if necessary) to the front of the bag, aligning the edges of the felt and stab stitching the pieces neatly together about ¼" (0.5 cm) from the edge all around (B). Then stitch the gusset to the back in the same way.

**2** Double over the strap lengthwise, and stitch the long sides together. Overcast the ends.

**3** Sew each end of the strap to the sides of the bag at the gusset. Stitching a neat square shape will help to strengthen the area (C).

**4** Mark the center point of the top of the bag on each side with tailor's chalk.

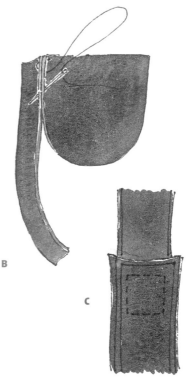

B

C

# make the buttons and loop

**1** Take a scrap of felt with colored layers (see page 40) and roll it into a Swiss-roll shape 1" (2.5 cm) in diameter and cut, as shown (D). Make a second roll, leaving a 5" (12 cm) tail at one end.

**2** Using a strong thread and large-eyed needle, stab stitch through the rolled up felt to secure it (E).

**3** Stitch the other end of the tail to the roll to make a loop.

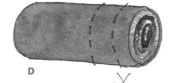

D

**4** Attach the button with the loop and the one without the loop to the top center of the front and back respectively of the bag at the marked points.

## MULTICOLORED FELT ROLLS

Layers of colored felt, rolled into cylinders. Slice across the rolls to create buttons.

E

# simple briefcase

This design makes a good briefcase shape, but it could also be used as a laptop computer case. Many people these days rely on a laptop—but the cases for them are expensive and, let's face it, very boring! Felt is the ideal material for creating a cover that will protect the laptop, helping to prevent it from getting damaged (if felt was good enough once upon a time for body armor, it is good enough for a laptop!). This version is very simple and classical so it is ideal for business use, but if you want a more personal version, then you can always create some extra decoration.

If you do use the case for a laptop, you will need to reinforce the handle area, ideally with a piece of leather stitched to the inside top.

## MATERIALS

7½ OZ (215 G) MERINO WOOL
TOP

FELTING EQUIPMENT (SEE
PAGE 34)

STRONG THREAD AND LARGE-
EYED NEEDLE

SNAP FASTENERS

LEATHER REINFORCEMENT
(FOR LAPTOP COVER)

### ALTERNATIVE DESIGN

You could make a similar bag
with a flap using seamless felt
(see pages 80–81), with
embroidery that links the flap
to the front of the bag.

# HOW TO MAKE IT

This briefcase is made from well-hardened flat felt. You will need
three thick layers of wool top to make a sufficiently durable and dense
fabric. If you want to use it for a laptop, then once the felting is
complete, you can cut out the pieces to the size of the laptop, allowing
a little extra all around for ease and shrinkage. The carrying handle
needs to be strong and very firmly secured for a laptop case, so
reinforce the handle inside with a piece of leather.

## making the felt

**1** Using the prepared work surface , mark
out the area for the size of felt required,
remembering to allow a little extra for
shrinkage. For the cover shown here, you
will need a piece roughly 38 by 20" (95 by
50 cm).

**2** Create the first layer of the felt, laying
the tufts of wool top side by side (A).

**3** To make the second layer, place the tufts
perpendicular to the first layer. To make a
third layer, lay the tufts down
perpendicular to the previous layer. Make
sure the layers are thickly covered.

**4** Felt and full the piece (see pages
35–36), but be prepared to rub it for
longer when you felt it, and roll it for
longer in the fulling to harden it
sufficiently. Rinse and dry well.

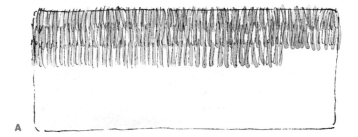

A

# cutting out the case

**1** Cut out one piece for the front and flap (21 by 12" [53 by 30 cm]) and one piece for the back (10 by 12" [25 by 30 cm]) plus two side gussets (10 by 2" [25 by 5 cm)] and one bottom gusset (12 by 2" [30 by 5 cm]), and one for the felt handle measuring [12 by 2" (30 by 5 cm)] wide (**B**).

**2** For the felt handle, you will need a piece 12 by 2" (30 by 5 cm) wide, doubled over and stitched with strong thread. **B**

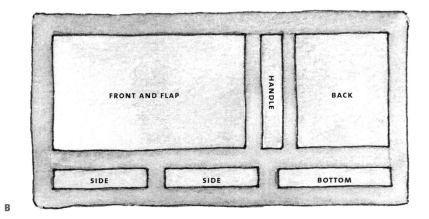

# stitching the case

**1** Lining up the pieces carefully, stitch one gusset to the front. Using a strong thread, stab stitch in position ½" (1 cm) from the edge (**c**).

**2** Stitch the gusset to the other side of the front panel (**D**).

**3** Stitch the other gusset to the front and back as in Steps 1 and 2.

**4** Stitch the base gusset to the base of the front, back and two side gussets, in the same way.

**5** Double over the handle and stitch in place with strong thread (or use a leather handle).

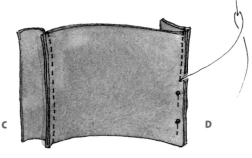

# making the handle

**1** Cut two slits just long enough to take the width of the strap on the shoulder of the case. Insert the handle, leaving about 2" (5 cm) at each end inside the bag. Overcast the ends in place (**E**).

**2** For a laptop case, reinforce this area with a piece of thin leather cut to the same size and backstitched (or machine stitched) in place (**F**).

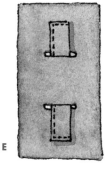

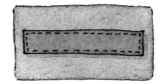

# decorative flat felt

Decorative or textured flat felt is similar in construction to plain felt, in that the layers of wool top are laid down and felted together, but additional interest is created by rubbing in small amounts of other wool top or different fibers, such as yarns or threads, into the final layers during the felting process.

You can also add small amounts of wool top to a fabric base, such as chiffon, silk, cheesecloth, or voile, to make a marvelously light and airy but durable fabric, which is ideal for scarves.

Some of the techniques used for decorative flat felt are also used in making seamless felt (see pages 78–117).

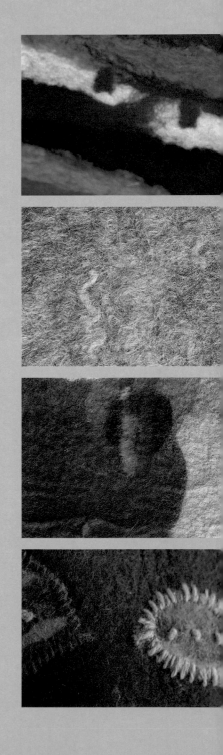

# MAKING DECORATIVE FLAT FELT

Decorative, or textured, felt is made like plain flat felt, but the addition of extra pieces of fleece or yarn, or indeed silk or muslin (according to the style), demands particular care during the felting process to ensure that they bond properly with the main pieces of fiber. To this end, when rubbing the felt, pay particular attention to any areas with spot decoration. The number of layers of felt, and the thickness, will vary according to the design of the project.

**MATERIALS**

**(FOR THREE-LAYERED PIECE OF FLAT FELT, 12" [30 CM] SQUARE):**

**ABOUT 2 OZ (60 G) OF MERINO WOOL TOP**

**YARNS OR ADDITIONAL WOOL TOP IN CONTRASTING COLORS**

**TOWEL**

**NET CURTAIN**

**RATTAN BLIND**

**WARM, SOAPY WATER**

**BAR OF SOAP**

**PAPER FOR TEMPLATES**

## creating the base

**1** Using the prepared work surface , take a a section of the wool top, and, holding it a good 5" (12 cm) from the end, pull out a tuft about 5" (12 cm) long (**A**) and smooth out the strands.

**2** Lay the first tuft down in one corner and then lay subsequent tufts side by side in a row (about 12 in/30 cm long in this case). Then make another row of tufts next to it, facing the same direction, and so on (**B**), until you have filled the square. This creates the first layer of felt.

**3** To make the second layer, lay down the next layer of tufts perpendicluar to the first layer (**A**).

A

# adding texture

You can now add any texture or decoration you wish to the third layer of felt. Lay down the third layer of tufts perpendicular to the previous layer. To create a similar pattern to the one shown, arrange small tufts of wool top in swirls and little pieces of thread on top of this third layer of tufts to complete the first stage (B).

B

# the felting process

**1** You can now wet the wool fiber to begin the process of felting them together. Cover the layers with a net curtain. Then, with the hand-hot, soapy water, wet the felt. Make sure you wet the entire area thoroughly but not to the point of it being awash. However, the wool should be distinctly wet, rather than simply damp. Press it flat with your hands.

**2** Taking the bar of soap, gently rub the surface of the net with it. Using the flats of your hands in a circular motion, exert just enough pressure to rub the fibers together without shifting the tufts of fleece (C).

**3** Once you have rubbed for about 15 minutes, you can check to see if the decoration (D) has meshed with the wool tops. Gently try to lift a piece of decoration. If it moves, you will need to continue the rubbing process.

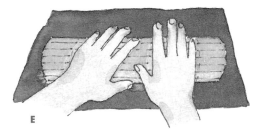

E

**5** Finally, full the felt (see page 36), rolling it backward and forward in a blind or mat for 10 minutes. Rinse and dry well (F).

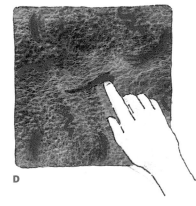

D

**4** Turn the piece over, wet the other side, and repeat Steps 1 to 3.

C

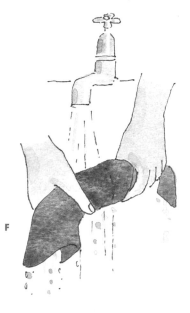

F

# zigzag muffler

You'll love this bright scarf design for its avant-garde attitude inspired by the zany color mix and offbeat shape. Feel free to use up any odds and ends that remain from your other felt projects, but keep the colors similar in saturation (color strength) to give the design cohesiveness; this particular scarf uses lots of clear, bright hues but you could just as easily make one using softer, more earthy shades. See a similar but more sophisticated version combining silk voile and wool top on pages 58–61. No preliminary work is needed—the scarf designs itself.

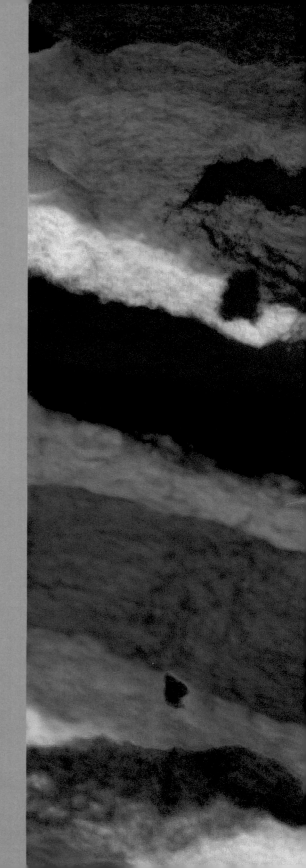

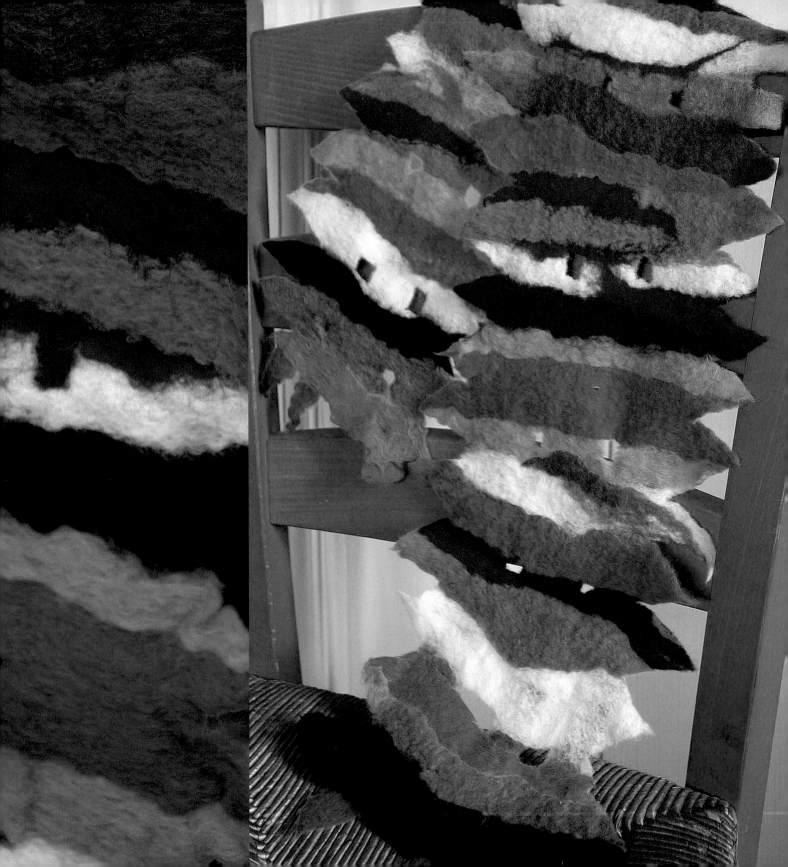

**MATERIALS**

ASSORTMENT OF WOOL TOP IN
VARIOUS COLORS

FELTING EQUIPMENT (SEE
PAGE 34)

SCISSORS

# HOW TO MAKE IT

No preliminary design work is needed for this scarf. It is made by creating three long bands of wool top with short bands of wool top laid across them. If you wish, you can make it from odds and ends of wool top left over from other projects. It looks best as a short scarf—worn like a muffler—doubled over.

# creating the design

**1** On a prepared work surface (see page 34) lay out the design for the scarf.

**2** First, make the backing for the scarf by laying out three 42" (105 cm) long strands of wool top. Leave a 4" (10 cm) gap between each strand. Then lay the colored horizontal bands of wool top across these strands. Tease out tufts of each color, about 8" (20 cm) long, and lay them side by side along the length of the scarf (**A**). The color mixture is your choice, but generally it is best to opt for strong color contrasts or shades of one color, as in the blue scarf opposite.

A

**3** Lay the net over the arranged layers and sprinkle with warm, soapy water until they are thoroughly wet but not waterlogged. Pat them down flat with your hands.

**4** Gently rub a bar of soap over the net, then rub with both hands, using a gentle polishing action. It is important not to move the fleeces, so be careful how you rub. Rub for 10 minutes and then turn the scarf over and repeat the process on the back. The fibers have bonded well enough if you can pick up the scarf in one piece.

# fulling the felt

**1** To make the scarf firmer and to ensure that all the horizontally laid wool top bond fully with the backing, roll the scarf (still in the net) around a stick or in a blind. Push it backward and forward for several minutes, changing direction as you do so (**B**).

**B**

**2** Untie the net and remove the scarf. Squeeze out the excess water. Rinse and dry well.

# finishing the design

**1** You can now cut away some of the felt, using sharp scissors, to trim the edges and ends, and create matching holes in the colored bands.

**2** Cut the ends of each of the colored bands to create a zigzag edge. Cut small holes in matching pairs for additional decoration (**c**).

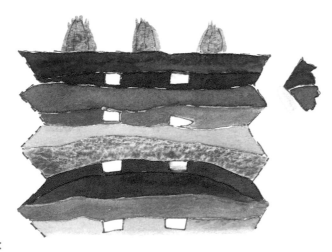

**C**

**ALTERNATIVE DESIGN**

**A similar design in shades of blue. The ends of the scarf are trimmed into rough points.**

# chiffon
# scarf

You can make marvelously delicate scarves using wool top in combination with fine fabrics, such as chiffon, cheesecloth, silk voile, or muslin. The making process is similar to using wool top alone, and in it the wool top and other fabrics are bonded together to create an entirely new fabric that varies in translucency according to the quantities of fine fabrics that are included. You can use the fabric as a backing for the wool top, or you can incorporate small pieces of fabric into the felting process. The scarves shown on these pages are made using different materials and varying construction methods. Once you understand the principles, you can create designs of your own.

**MATERIALS**

SILK CHIFFON, 50
   BY 10" (125 BY 25 CM)

⅓ OZ (10 G) WOOL TOP

BUBBLEWRAP

FELTING EQUIPMENT (SEE
   PAGE 34)

SCISSORS

# HOW TO MAKE IT

The Chiffon and Zigzag scarves are both made using a combination of fleece with chiffon. In the scarf shown on page 59, the bands of wool top are laid widthwise onto a backing fabric (as shown in the following instructions). In the scarf shown opposite, the bands of wool top are laid lengthwise down the scarf on the backing fabric, and cut to the measurements required. This scarf measures 50 by 10" (125 by 25 cm).

## creating the design

**1** Lay out the bubblewrap on the work surface with the bubbles on top. On half the width of the bubblewrap, lay down the silk chiffon (or other chosen fabric).

**2** Tease out the tufts of wool top, about 10" (25 cm) long, and lay them down at intervals across the ground fabric. Keep the pieces thin and well teased out. The scarf should be very light and airy (**A**).

**3** Sprinkle with warm, soapy water and then fold the remaining width of bubblewrap over the fabric, trapping the scarf inside the two layers of bubblewrap.

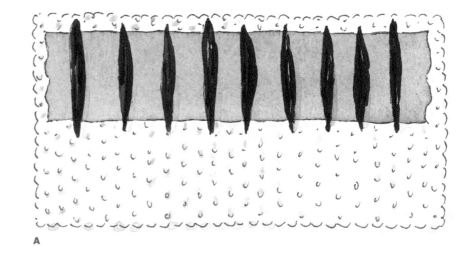

**A**

**4** Press down all over to distribute the water evenly, taking care not to shift the fibers.

# fulling the scarf

**1** Carefully roll the strip of bubblewrap containing the scarf around a stick and tie in a couple of places to keep everything in place.

**2** Now roll the stick backward and forward for about 15 minutes, using a lot of pressure. A towel laid on the work surface will help prevent it from slipping. Change the rolling direction to ensure even felting.

**3** From time to time, open up the package to check if the fibers have bonded together properly. If not, continue with the rolling.

**4** Once the fibers have bonded, remove the scarf from the package and rinse it in cold water. Dry it flat overnight.

**ALTERNATIVE DESIGN**

This scarf is made using the same process, but in this design three bands of wool top are positioned vertically down the scarf, rather than horizontally across it. Simply pull out long strands of fiber from the wool top and lay them on the ground fabric.

# table runner

Table runners have long been popular in Scandinavian countries and have made their way into global home-decorating plans. They make a striking addition to a long wooden table or sideboard. You're sure to dream up all kinds of different decorations, but the more muted designs and colorways look best in modern interiors. This design in soft gray Merino wool top has touches of bright and softer blue rubbed in to it. Patterns that emphasize the length of the design look most attractive, and wavy, randomly positioned patterns are easier to create.

**MATERIALS**

13 OZ (370 G) MERINO WOOL TOP

BRIGHT BLUE WOOL TOP AND BRIGHT BLUE KNITTING YARN (PURE WOOL ONLY)

FELTING EQUIPMENT (SEE PAGE 34)

# HOW TO MAKE IT

This table runner measures 44 by 19" (110 by 46 cm). It is created from three layers of Merino wool top, with some pure bright blue pieces of wool and yarn for decoration. If you want a thinner, more delicate runner, use only two layers of Merino wool top. You could use this design just as easily for a rug, but lay down a couple of extra layers of wool top. An alternative rug design is shown opposite.

## making the base

Make the first two layers of felt (as shown on pages 34–36). Tease out the tufts of wool and lay them down carefully, so that they are just overlapping (**A**). The more evenly you create the layers, the flatter and more even the finished felt will be.

A

## adding the decoration

**1** Once you have laid down the first two layers, you are ready to make the final decorative layer. To do this you need to lay down the third layer of wool top perpendicular to the previous layer. Then add the small strands of blue wool top at intervals (**B**).

B

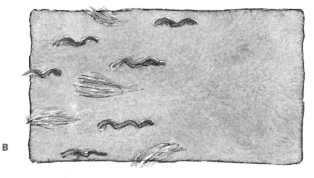

**2** Snip off the pieces of yarn, a few inches in length, and lay them down at intervals.

**3** Cover the whole piece with net and sprinkle with water. Press flat. Draw soap over the wetted area and  rub gently for as long as is necessary to ensure that the small strands of wool are felted into the top layer. Add more soap and water as necessary.

## fulling the felt

**1** Once the decoration has bonded to the top layer of wool, roll the piece up in a rattan blind or around a stick, tie it up, and roll it backward and forward.

**2** After 10 minutes or so, undo the piece and check to see if the felt has hardened and shrunk. If it has, proceed to the next step; if not continue rollling for a little longer.

**3** Rinse out all soap (until water runs clear) and leave it to dry.

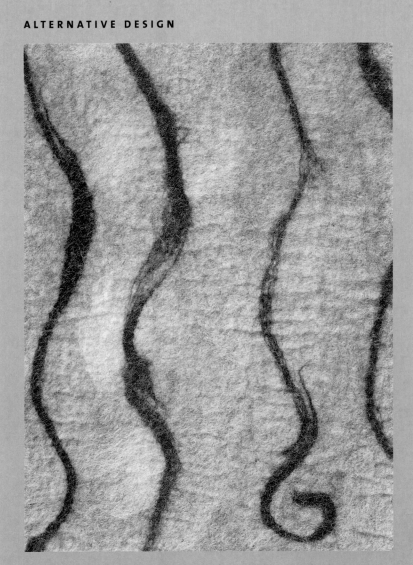

**ALTERNATIVE DESIGN**

This could be used for a runner or for a rug (as could the design for the runner shown on these pages). To create a rug, allow an extra layer or so in the felt-making process for durability or make the individual layers thicker. You will need a greater quantity of wool top.

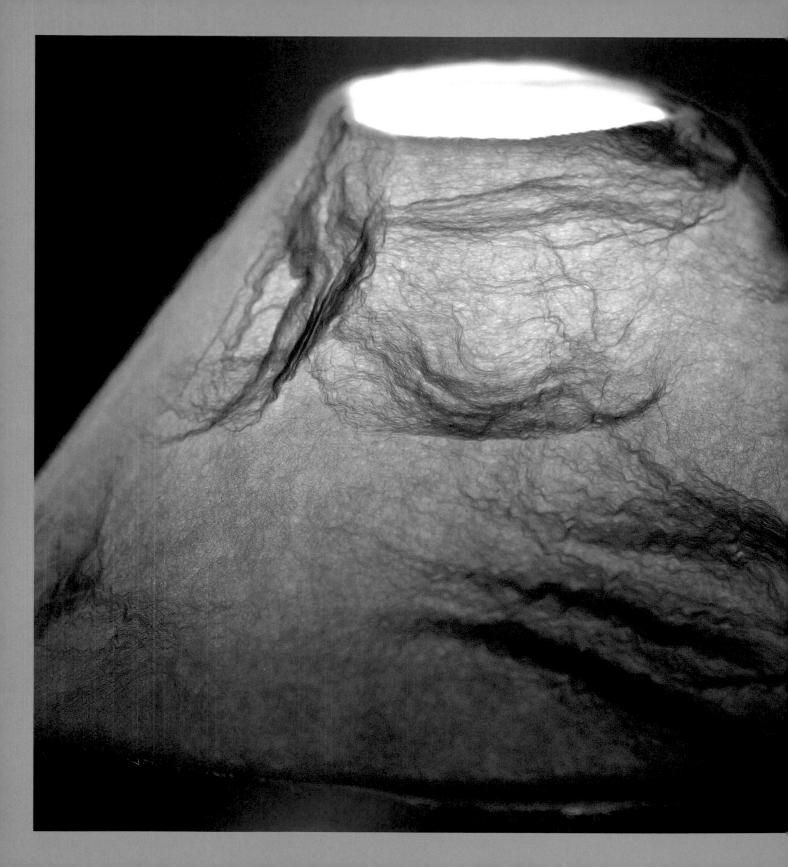

# silk inlaid lampshade

Surprise—felt is a great material for lampshades! If you use textured felt, as here, the varying thickness allows more or less light to show through, giving an attractively dappled effect. It is best to apply the felt to an existing inexpensive shade.

This lampshade is made from two fine layers of felt, the top layer incorporating a swirling pattern in tussah silk for a very delicate textural effect. A similar throw, made using the same technique but incorporating lines of bouclé yarns, is shown on page 69.

**MATERIALS**

½ OZ (15 G) MERINO
WOOL TOP

TUSSAH SILK TOP

FELTING EQUIPMENT (SEE
PAGE 34)

PLAIN WHITE LAMPSHADE

NEEDLE AND MATCHING
THREAD (OR HOT GLUE
GUN)

SCISSORS

# HOW TO MAKE IT

This lampshade measures 9" (23 cm ) in diameter by 6" (15 cm) deep. You will need a piece of felt measuring 35" (87.5 cm) by the depth to cover it (use a piece of string around the shade base to measure yours). The shade shown here is made from a piece of fine, flat felt, consisting of two layers: tussah silk has been included in a swirling pattern in the second layer. You could use a similar technique to create a delicate throw for a sofa or chair. Alternatively, for either the shade or the throw, use lines of threads instead of the silk. In both cases, make sure the decorative threads bond fully during the felting process with the underlying layers of wool top.

## making the felt

**1** Prepare the work surface (see page 34) and measure out the area for the size of felt that you need, plus a little extra for shrinkage.

**2** Tease out the wool top to create the first layer, laying the tufts down side by side in rows.

**3** To make the second layer, lay tufts of wool top down perpendicular to the first layer. Over these, lay down swirls of tussah silk in a random pattern (A).

**4** Check that you have covered the area, and that the edges in particular are well covered. Then cover with a net and start the wetting process (see page 35).

**5** Once the wool top and the silk have bonded, you can start the fulling process. Roll the piece around a stick or in a blind (see page 36) and roll backward and forward for about 10 minutes. Check to see if the piece has felted. If not, continue the process. Otherwise, rinse out and hang to dry.

A

# finishing the shade

**1** Cut a single piece of felt long enough to go around the circumference of the base and wide enough to cover the depth of the shade (B).

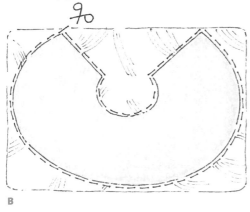

B

**2** Secure the felt to the shade, either with dabs of glue (a hot glue gun is ideal) or by stitching the ends together (c).

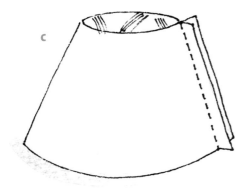

C

**3** Finally, turn the shade right side out, put it over the existing shade, and trim it top and bottom to fit.

**ALTERNATIVE THROW**

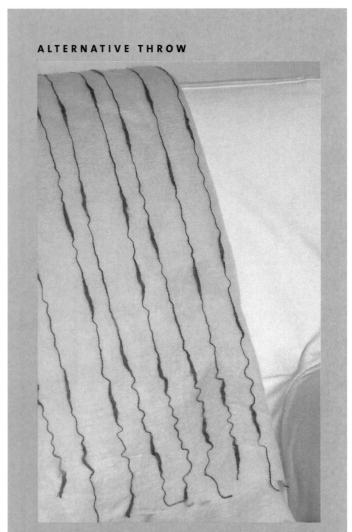

If you wish, you can make a very similar piece of lightweight fine felt for a throw. Simply increase the size of the piece (and the quantities of wool top and tussah silk proportionally). For an alternative design, use similar, creamy colored Merino wool top in two layers but add rows of neutral bouclé threads in randomly placed stripes in the second layer. Then felt it (see pages 34–36).

# patchwork runner

Inspired by a Bauhaus woven rug made in the 1920s, this runner is made using wool top that has been dyed with natural dyes to create soft, harmonizing colors. Although the design looks complex, it is not a particularly difficult piece to make. However, you do need to ensure that you rub the felt long and hard enough so that all the fibers mesh together properly, while taking care that you do not shift them around as you rub.

**MATERIALS**

6 oz (185 g) of dark blue Merino wool top

3 oz (90 g) naturally dyed combed Merino wool top (dyeing instructions are given on page 122)

felting equipment (see page 34)

# HOW TO MAKE IT

This panel is a little different from the other projects in that it uses naturally dyed Merino wool top. You can, of course, use chemically dyed top, but the softness of the colors in this piece stems from natural dyes. The natural-dye colors (see page 122) do not involve lots of harsh mordants. You will be surprised and pleased at the range of shades you can achieve from a single dye bath. You may not want to copy this design exactly, but the aim is to ensure a harmonious balance of color, with no single shade jumping out from the others— so use colors with similar saturation values (deepness or lightness of tone). Varying the size of the patches adds to the charm.

## creating the design

1 Make two layers of dark blue wool top for the backing in the usual way (see Making flat felt on pages 34–35).

2 On top of the second layer, lay the colors by putting down the pink, orange, and yellow shapes first and then fillling in the other colors between them (A).

3 Cover with a net, sprinkle with warm water and, using olive oil soap as necessary, rub for about 15 minutes or until the wool tops are well bonded.

A

# finishing

When the fibers are well bonded, place the piece in a blind, add hot water, and roll well for about 10 minutes or until the panel has hardened. Then rinse well and hang to dry.

**Above: The finished design laid out before felting.**
**Right: A detail showing a section of the patchwork in which the patches have been overlaid and felted in.**

# bucket bag

Made out of sheets of flat felt with a rolled handle, this bag is a classic, and is a very popular design. Use a single color to keep it simple, or you can embellish one or both sides of the bag with little stitched-on or rubbed-in patches of textured felt. You could also make the handles a different color from the bag.

This particular bag was made from pure Merino wool top. The top comes in a wonderful range of colors, so you can be sure to find shades to match your wardrobe.

**MATERIALS**

9 OZ (275 G) OF MERINO
WOOL TOP

BASIC FELT EQUIPMENT (SEE
PAGE 34)

FELTING NEEDLE AND THREADS

TEXTURED FELT FOR PATCHES

TAILOR'S CHALK

RIBBON FOR HANDLE BACKING

# HOW TO MAKE IT

This bag is made from a single piece of plain flat felt, three layers thick, with two rolled felt handles. The front of the bag has been decorated with randomly sized and positioned patches of decorative felt that are stitched onto it or rubbed in (see page 53), but you could leave the whole bag plain. Make the felt for the bag first, cut out the pattern pieces, make the handles, and cut and stitch the little decorative patches to the front of the bag. Stitch the bag and add the handles—what could be easier?

## cutting out the bag

This bag is made from five main pieces of plain felt—a front and back, both identical, two sides and a base—plus two handles. It measures 9" (25 cm) wide by 9" (25 cm) deep, narrowing to 6" (15 cm) at the base. You will need two pattern pieces (front and back), two side pieces and a base (see page 125). The handles are a simple rolled felt design (see opposite). The little patches that decorate one side of the bag are small irregular shapes, an inch or two in diameter, cut either from a piece of inlaid felt or from the same felt as the bag and randomly positioned on the bag front. They are then whipstitched onto the bag using contrasting colored yarns.

**1** Cut out the pattern for the bag from page 125 (or your own design) and transfer it to templates.

**2** Make a three-layered piece of felt (see pages 34–36) measuring about 20 by 30" (50 by 75 cm) after felting.

**3** Lay the templates on the felt, mark around the edges with tailor's chalk, and cut two the same for the front/back, two the same for the sides, and one for the base (**A**). Use a pair of scissors to cut the felt.

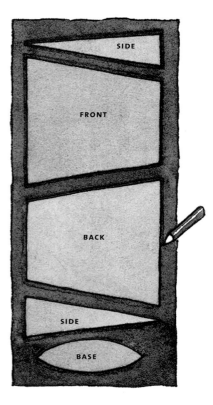

A

## making the handles

The handles consist of two pieces of rolled felt. The ones shown here are made from a single color, but if you wish you can create a striped handle by joining two or more layers of top together.

**1** Lay down a strand of the wool top (about 15" [38 cm] long) on the work surface. Wet your hands and soap them thoroughly, then sprinkle water on the wool and roll it backward and forward, as if making a pottery coil.

**2** Keep rolling and wetting the felt until it thickens and forms a neat sausage shape, about 24" (61 cm) long (**B**). Once it is the required length and thickness, allow the felt to dry.

**3** Cut into two pieces of equal length, 12" (30 cm) long, to make the two handles for the bag.

B

## making the bag

**1** Stitch the bag front to the sides, using a felting needle and matching colored tapestry wool and stab stitch to create raised seams about ¼" (.5 cm) from the edge of the felt (**C**). Stitch the bag back to the sides in the same way, and finally stitch the base to the sides, back and front.

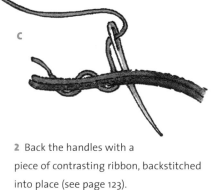

C

**2** Back the handles with a piece of contrasting ribbon, backstitched into place (see page 123).

**3** Mark the postions for the handles at points equidistant along the top back and front of the bag. Pin and then backstitch the handles to the bag. Overcast with chain stitches (**D**).

D

**BAG DECORATION**

If you wish, you can make some textured patches to apply to the bag. Cut out randomly shaped pieces of textured felt and whipstitch them, using contrasting colored yarn, to the bag front.

# seamless
# felt

The projects in this chapter are all made with what is termed a "resist"—a piece of plastic that prevents two layers of wool fibers from felting together, so the resulting piece of felt, when the resist is removed, is seamless. Felting with a resist is the ideal choice for projects such as slippers and hats, a tea cozy, a bag or purse—no stitching is involved. It is a particularly useful technique for working with thick felt, as stitching through the thicknesses can be time-consuming and difficult.

Most any kind of plastic can be used to make the resist. You could use a heavy-duty garbage can liner or bubblewrap, but bear in mind the resist needs to be flexible enough to be rolled up with the felt.

This form of felt making is more advanced than simple flat felt, as you need to ensure the layers and edges are evenly felted.

# MAKING SEAMLESS FELT

Set up your work surface in the same way as you do for making flat felt (see pages 34–36), but in addition to the usual equipment you will need a suitable template as a resist—normally a sheet of heavy-duty plastic—that prevents the layers of wool tops from bonding together. The wool top is laid down on both sides of the resist, building up layers in the same way as with flat felt. Once the wool top has been felted down enough so that it holds its shape, one edge of the felted piece can be cut, the resist removed, and the final felting can then take place.

The cut area forms the opening (or openings) for the felted project, such as a container, tea cozy, or hat.

## creating the first layers

**1** Cut out a plastic resist to the shape required. Remember to allow an extra 1" (2.5 cm) all around for shrinkage.

**2** Lay the resist on the prepared work surface and tease out tufts about 5" (12 cm) long and lay them side by side on the template, overlapping the edges of the template by about 1" (2.5 cm) (A).

**3** Cover with the net and sprinkle with warm, soapy water. Press flat. Remove net, turn the resist over and fold edges of wool tops onto the plastic. Repeat Step 2.

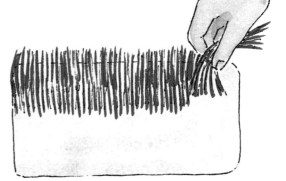

A

### MATERIALS

(FOR A THREE-LAYERED
PIECE OF SEAMLESS FELT
15 BY 6" [38 BY 15 CM]):

ABOUT 2 OZ (60 G) OF
MERINO WOOL TOP

OLD TOWEL

NET CURTAIN

RATTAN BLIND

WARM, SOAPY WATER

BAR OF SOAP

PLASTIC RESIST

# felting the design

1 Create a second layer with the top perpendicular to the previous layer (B), and repeat previous Step 4.

2 If required, create a third layer, again perpendicular to the previous layer, on both sides. Add any required design by laying down small tufts of colors, on one or both sides as desired.

3 Cover the finished shape with a net and sprinkle with warm water. Press flat. Gently rub soap over the net and then rub with both hands in a polishing movement (c) for about 10 minutes. Turn the shape over and repeat the process on the other side.

# fulling the felt

1 Once the felt has shrunk to the desired size, you can remove the resist by cutting along the side that will form the eventual opening, using a sharp pair of scissors.

2 You can now finish the felting process (see page 36) by rolling the felt in a blind or on a stick, and rolling it backward and forward (for 10 to 15 minutes) until the felt hardens, periodically wetting the felt with very hot water.

3 Check the size from time to time and roll as required in different directions to achieve the desired shape and size. You will also need to work the seam areas with your fingers to achieve a rounded shape.

4 Finally rinse the felt until all the soapy water is removed. Allow to dry.

# slippers

Imagine slipping your feet into soft clouds . . . that's the sensation you'll get from these cozy, toasty handmade felt slippers. Use colorful dyed Merino wool top or a mixture using wool from sheep like Romney, Icelandic, Finn, or Polwarth, whose wool is strong and soft.

Before you start, think about the type of slipper you want to make and then match the felt thickness to your choice. For a simple backless mule, the felt must be thick and firm to hold the shape without flopping. For a Turkish-style slipper, the felt can be thinner. The slippers shown on these pages are made using a boot-shaped template (see page 124) and the felt is then cut to suit your slipper choice.

## MATERIALS

3½ oz (105 g) Merino
    wool top

A few pieces of
    contrasting Merino
    wool top for the
    decoration

Plastic resist

Felting equipment (see
    page 34)

Scissors

# HOW TO MAKE IT

These slippers have been made with a few strands of contrasting fibers worked into the uppers to provide an interesting pattern, but you can even more easily make a plain pair or, if you prefer, create spots of color in the lining (see page 86) instead. The resist used in making the slippers is a single boot-shaped piece, with a left and right foot. The slippers are then cut and shaped to size after being felted. The slippers shown here are a women's medium size with a rounded toe. For a man's medium size, increase the quantities of wool top by about 25 percent.

## making the slippers

1 Draw around the outline of your feet (or those of the person for whom the slippers are being made) on a piece of paper (A). Cut this out and then use the template for the pair of slippers on page 124 to cut out the plastic resist, allowing a couple of inches all around for ease and shrinkage. You will need a left- and right-foot pattern.

2 Place the resist on the work surface, and lay down the wool top on the resist (see page 80). For these slippers, three layers were used.

A

3 Cover one side of the resist with a similar weight and density of fibers, laid down in rows, side by side, facing in the same direction. Allow the fibers to spread out a little over the edges of the resist pattern as shown opposite.

4 When one side is covered, cover with a net, sprinkle with warm water, and pat the fibers down. Turn over the resist, and fold the fibers onto the plastic. Cover this side as in Step 3.

**5** If you are using a second color, repeat Steps 2 and 3 to create the second layer (B).

**6** Finally lay down the third layer in the same way, adding any decoration you might like. In this case, lay wavy lines of contrasting wool top down on the uppers and small swirls of mixed colors along the sides of the slippers (as shown in C) before wetting the fibers.

B

## the felting process

**1** Follow the felting steps (see page 35), rubbing for about 10 minutes on the first side, and 10 minutes on the second side. By now the fleece will have started to shrink and will be pulling on the plastic shape. Rub for a little longer, paying particular attention to the edges to ensure that they have felted evenly. (It is easy in felting to ignore the sides leading to weak, thin felt at these points.)

**2** Draw a line at the mid-center point of the pattern (C), between the two feet, and cut through the felt to remove the resist and create two separate slipper shapes.

**3** You can now harden the felt, by rolling the slippers in a blind or around a stick. Using very hot water, roll backward and forward for 10 minutes or so, in each direction, until the felt has hardened.

**4** Remove the resist and further full the slippers by hand, rounding out the seam areas. Squeeze out any excess water, rinse and hang out to dry.

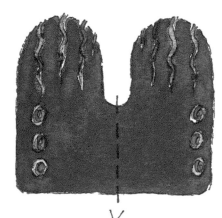

C

## finishing the slippers

**1** Cut the uppers and backs of the slippers into their final shape—in this case with a squared-off vamp (D).

**2** Add any further decoration, such as a bow (see page 87), using scraps from the vamp.

D

## MATERIALS

2 OZ (70 G) PALE GRAY
MERINO WOOL TOP
(INSIDE LAYER)

4½ OZ (140 G) MID-GRAY
COMBED WOOL TOP (TOP
LAYER AND SPOTS)

PLASTIC RESIST

FELTING EQUIPMENT (SEE
PAGE 34)

SCISSORS

# SPOTTED SLIPPERS

Adding spots to the lining for your slippers gives them a splash of color and personality. Follow the steps for the slippers on pages 84–85, but add the contrasting spots directly onto the resist, before the first layer of pale gray top. Then add the next two layers of wool top (here in mid-gray, but choose any hue you like). Cut the slipper top after fulling into the chosen shape.

**1** Follow the steps for the adult slippers, but add the contrasting spots first on the resist, before laying down the inside color (in this case the pale gray).

**2** Then add the next two layers of wool top as in the instructions on pages 84–85. Follow the usual felting instructions and cut the vamp into the desired shape.

# CHILDREN'S SLIPPERS

Keep your baby or child's toes safe and warm in these cozy slippers. Cut the pattern on page 124 with a more pointed toe to suit the size required and follow steps on pages 84–85 (with a contrasting lining). The pair of little booties shown fit a small baby. For a toddler, remember to increase the quantities of wool top. Use a piece of the leftover felt to make the little twist ties on the front of the slippers.

**MATERIALS**

½ OZ (15 G) RED MERINO WOOL TOP

½ OZ (15 G) ORANGE MERINO WOOL TOP

PLASTIC RESIST

FELTING EQUIPMENT (SEE PAGE 34)

SCISSORS

**1** Cut out an appropriately sized template for the resist, and lay down the layers of wool top in the usual way.

**2** To finish the slippers, do not cut the vamp down, but leave the bootie shape. From a scrap of felt, make a little tie twist as decoration, stitched to the front of the slipper, or cut the front center of the vamp and fold back each side to make a cuff.

# inlaid
# containers

These little containers are created from Merino wool top, with a simple yarn inlay running around the top and base of the containers. You can make several in varying sizes and shapes and with minor differences in the pattern to create a small group. The simpler the style and the pattern, the more effective the form will be. The group shown here comprises two taller shapes and one smaller, rounded form. A more organically shaped variation of these is shown on page 91.

You can use them as little sculptural objects in their own right or fill them with small odds and ends.

MATERIALS

1 OZ (25 G) MERINO
WOOL TOP (FOR THREE
    CONTAINERS)

BOUCLÉ YARN FOR THE INLAY

PLASTIC RESIST

FELTING EQUIPMENT (SEE
    PAGE 34)

SCISSORS OR SCALPEL

# HOW TO MAKE IT

These little containers are very easy to make. For the tall containers, you can use either a plastic resist or a mold (such as a small flowerpot). For the circular containers, you simply need a circular template, such as a saucer. The instructions here are given for the two styles of container, each using a resist. The taller container measures 5 by 3" (12.5 by 8 cm) and the round one is 5" (12.5 cm) in diameter, but you can choose the size to suit your purpose. The decoration in each case consists of bands of contrasting yarn. An alternative version is shown opposite.

## creating the design

**1** You will first need to create the templates for the container shapes. Each template should be cut to the height and width of the chosen shape, with 1" (2.5 cm) all around to allow for shrinkage. Lay the templates on the plastic resist, and cut out the shapes (A).

**2** Using a prepared work surface, tease out tufts of wool top about 4" (10 cm) long. Lay them on the plastic resists, side by side, until the shapes are covered, allowing the tops to overlap the edges of the resist slightly (B). Cover with a net curtain, sprinkle with water, and press flat.

**3** Remove the net, turn each covered resist over, and fold the overlapping edges of wool onto the plastic. Then lay down a layer of wool in the same way as in the previous step. You will have now have covered both sides of the resist in the same way.

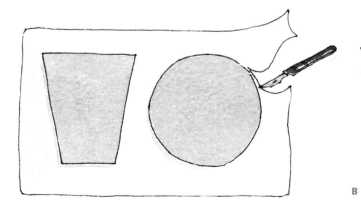

A

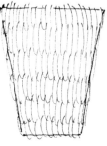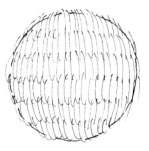

B

**4** Now create two more layers in the same way, but laying down each layer perpendicular to the previous layer (as shown on pages 34–36).

## adding the threads

**1** You can now lay down the threads on the top layer of felt. Position them as you wish on the design, in rows at the top or at the bottom of the containers or around the center of the circle (**C**). Wet the fibers, cover with the net and press flat with your hands. Repeat on the other side.

C

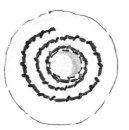

**2** Rub for 10 minutes on each side. Check to make sure that the threads have bonded with the fibers. Then cut an opening in each container (at the top of the cylinder and in the center of the circle), and remove the resist from each.

## fulling the felt

Roll the containers around a stick and tie in the usual way. Roll backward and forward for around 10 minutes, changing directions. Remove and work the shapes with your fist to round them out. Rinse well and leave to dry. Stuff the bowl with paper or cloth towels to help retain its shape while drying.

### ALTERNATIVE CONTAINERS

These organically shaped containers are made in a similar way to the round container shown, using a circular template, and turquoise or lime green Merino wool top. The contrasting colored decoration swirls out from the center of the circle. Work the shapes around your fist (after fulling around a stick) to achieve the organic shape. When the center is cut, a little flap at the top of each container is folded over and stitched down with a bead.

# tea cozy

Felt is fabulous as an insulating cover. The tea cozy shown here will fit over a standard-sized teapot, but it is very easy to adapt the shape to fit a favorite pot.

The decoration on the cozy is created from a recycled sweater, but you could use any kinds of inlaid threads or wool top, or you could embroider the front with a simple stitched outline. The inside of the cover is a delicious deep rust color.

A very similar shape forms the basic pattern for a simple holdall, shown on pages 96–97.

## MATERIALS

1½ oz (40 g) of one color (outside color) Merino wool top

¾ oz (20 g) in second color (inside color) Merino wool top

Scraps of striped knitting

Plastic resist

Felting equipment (see page 34)

Scissors

# HOW TO MAKE IT

This tea cozy has a pared-down shape, with a touch of decoration in the form of little strips of complementary colored knitting (no need to machine-wash it so that the fabric is fulled (see page 12) and won't fray when you cut it. For this particular design, the inside is in a contrasting color, but you can make all the layers the the same color if you prefer. The decorative knitted strips can adorn one or both sides of the cozy; the instructions that follow show them on both sides. Make the little tuffed handle from extra strips of felt.

## creating the design

1 Make a template to fit the shape of your teapot. You can make it with a semi-circular top, as shown here (using a large plate for the rounded top and extending the sides to fit your particular teapot). Cut out the plastic resist to the required shape and size, allowing a good 1" (2.5 cm) all around for ease and also allowing 1" (2.5 cm) or more all around for shrinkage (A).

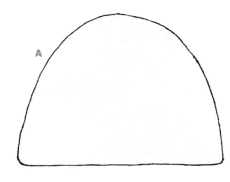

2 Cut out three narrow strips, each measuring ½ by 3" (1 by 8 cm) from the striped knitting and set aside (B).

3 Prepare the work surface (see page 34) and lay the resist on it.

# creating the layers

**1** Take the wool top tufts for one side of the cozy and lay them on the resist side by side, all facing in the same direction, and overlapping the edges of the resist in (see page 80).

**2** Cover with the net, sprinkle with warm, soapy water and press flat. Remove the net, and turn the resist over, folding over the edges of wool top (**c**). Repeat on this side of the resist.

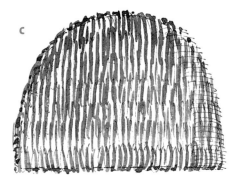

**To make the second layer**
Repeat Steps 1 and 2, laying down the wool top perpendicular to the previous layer.

**To make the final layer**
This is the top color of the cozy. Using the contrasting-colored wool top, repeat the steps for the first layer.

# felting the cozy

**1** Take the strips of knitting and place them on one side of the prepared cozy, taking care to position the center piece in the center of the cozy.

**2** Cover with the net, rub with soap, and press the shapes into the felt with your fingers.

**3** Felt the cozy (see page 35). Remove the net, check that the shapes are in place, and repeat the rubbing process on the other side until the felt is firm.

**4** Cut along the bottom edge of the cozy (**D**), and remove the resist. Roll the shape up in the rattan blind or tie it around a stick. Using hot water, roll the piece backward and forward for about 10 minutes, until the felted piece has shrunk sufficiently (check every few minutes). When the piece is the right size, remove it from the stick or blind, full the seam areas by hand, rinse, and allow to dry.

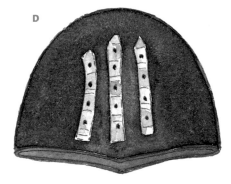

# making the handle

Cut a slice from the base of the cozy, and divide into three pieces Make a small cut in the top of the cozy, and insert the pieces through the cut. Backstitch (see page 122) into place (**E**).

**MATERIALS**

**2 OZ (60 G) OF MERINO
    WOOL TOP**

**SMALL QUANTITIES OF
    CONTRASTING-COLORED
    WOOL TOP**

**PLASTIC RESIST**

**FELTING EQUIPMENT (SEE
    PAGE 34)**

**PINS, NEEDLE AND THREAD**

**BAG HANDLE**

# HOW TO MAKE IT

This simple holdall bag is, in fact, little more than a variation on the tea cozy shown on the previous pages. Make it in the same way with three layers of felt around a rectangular resist which has rounded corners at the base. This bag measures around 12 by 10" (30 by 25 cm). An inexpensive handle, incorporated by folding over a section of the top and stitching it down, transforms the shape into a holdall bag. One side of the bag is decorated with a radiating sunburst design in contrasting-colored wool top. For a more minimalist approach, you could skip the handle and simply cut a rectangular slit about 1" (2.5 cm) from the top of the bag. You can create a contrasting-colored lining if you wish, adding the color when you lay down the first layer.

## creating the design

**1** Cut out a template resist for the bag from plastic. Cover the resist with three layers of wool top (see pages 80–81), laid down in the usual way (**A**), with each subsequent layer perpendicular to the former. Sprinkle with warm, soapy water at each stage.

**2** On the final layer, lay down the desired pattern (in this case a sunburst design). Cover with a net curtain, sprinkle with water, and rub well to ensure the design has bonded to the under layer.

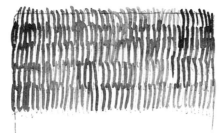

**A**

**3** Then felt the bag (see pages 35–36). Cut the opening and remove the resist (**B**). Work the seam areas by hand to round them out. Rinse and dry.

**B**

### Finishing the bag

Turn over the edge at the top of the bag on each side to incorporate the handle. Slip the bottom edge of each handle into position, and pin in place. Then overcast neatly around the edge (c).

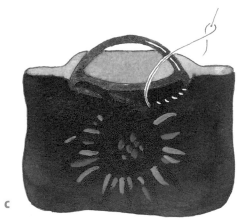

c

# cloche hat

You'll find it easy to make hats using the resist technique. In fact, this is the traditional way to create any hat shape. We have chosen to create two simple hat shapes; one is a pull-down soft cloche, a shape that is universally flattering and has been popular since the 1920s. The other is based on the traditional fez shape in the form of a simple pillbox.

The shape and form of the hat you choose to make will determine the form of the felt. For the cloche, very thin layers of felt have been used for maximum flexibility. For the fez, thick layers of felt, well-felted down to make the pillbox shape, are required. You can decorate these hat shapes in various ways. The cloche would look very pretty with the addition of a felted flower corsage on one side. For the fez, a traditional tassel provides the finishing touch.

**MATERIALS**

**1 OZ (30 G) MERINO WOOL TOP**

**TUSSAH SILK FOR DECORATION**

**FELTING EQUIPMENT (SEE PAGE 34)**

**PLASTIC RESIST**

**TAPE MEASURE**

**SCISSORS**

# HOW TO MAKE A CLOCHE

This hat has a very flattering shape, which suits most people, young or old. Once you have created the basic "bell" (the word *cloche* is French for bell) shape in fine, soft felt, you can cut the hat shape to achieve different brim styles. Dress the hat up for special occasions with a flower corsage pinned to one side, or add different fibers to the wool to create interesting textures. This hat has a tussah silk decoration incorporated in the top layer, but you could also use bouclé threads in rows around the base, for example, as shown on the containers on pages 88–91.

## making a cloche hat

**1** Ask a friend to measure the circumference of your head (just above your ears) or measure the diameter of an existing hat that fits.

**2** Cut the bell-shaped template (see page 125) from plastic, enlarging or reducing it as necessary on a photocopier. Remember to add 1" (2.5 cm) all around to allow for shrinkage (**A**).

**3** Lay down the first layer of wool top on one side of the plastic, making sure that the edges overlap a little. Cover with the net curtain, sprinkle with warm, soapy water, and wet the wool thoroughly.

**4** Turn the shape over and fold the edges onto the plastic. Lay down a layer of tufts of wool on this side of the resist as before, overlapping the edges again. Sprinkle with warm, soapy water as before, turn over, and fold over the edges.

**A**

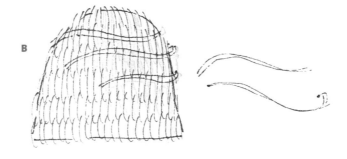

**5** Create a further layer on each side of the plastic, but laying the tufts perpendicular to the first layer, repeating Steps 3 and 4, and adding the swirls of tussah silk on both sides (**B**).

# felting the hat

**1** Cover the hat with the net curtain and wet it thoroughly with warm soapy water before beginning to rub the wool, using a polishing action with both hands. Do this for 10 minutes on one side, and then turn the shape over and repeat on the other side. The wool will have begun to shrink and will be starting to pull on the plastic.

**2** Cut along the base of the plastic resist, and remove it (**C**). The hat should now be well felted inside and out.

**3** Shape the hat over your fist, and full the hat further, paying particular attention to the seam areas, to ensure the hat has a rounded form.

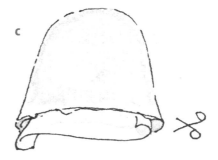

# finishing the hat

**1** Roll the hat in a rattan blind or wrap it around a stick, tied in a couple of places with tape.

**2** Now pour on very hot water and roll the blind backward and forward for a few minutes. Turn the blind at right angles and roll again for several more minutes.

**3** Remove the hat from the blind or stick, squeeze out excess water, and try the hat on. If it is too large, return it to the blind or stick and repeat the rolling steps for a minute or so, before opening and trying it on again.

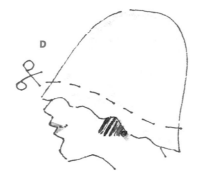

**4** Rinse the hat well in cold water and put it over an upturned bowl to dry.

### trimming the brim
The brim will have a loose, uneven edge. Cut some of the felt away (**D**), to create a neater, more balanced shape.

# HOW TO MAKE A PILLBOX HAT

**MATERIALS**

2½ oz (75 g) of Merino
    wool top

TAPE MEASURE

CARDBOARD, CLEAR TAPE
    AND PLASTIC WRAP FOR
    MOLD

FELTING EQUIPMENT (SEE
    PAGE 34)

NEEDLE AND YARNS FOR
    TASSEL

SCISSORS

The pillbox design stems from the fez, traditional headgear from Egypt and Turkey, and is adorned by a typical tassel, in purple and orange wool, stitched to the center of the crown. The hat is made from thick layers of felt, with an additional layer around the brim alone. The brim will need to be trimmed after felting, to ensure it has an even, solid edge (you could change the design by making the brim less deep). You could also make the hat more dressy by attaching a corsage flower to the center crown, or to one side of the hat, instead of the tassel. Alternatively, stitch a fine twisted braid around the edge of the crown where it joins the brim.

## creating the design

1 You will first need to make a mold for the hat out of cardboard. Measure your head (or ask a friend to help) just above the ears to get the correct size. Remember to add 1" (2.5 cm) to the size for shrinkage and cut out the sides of the hat and the crown. Make a circle to these measurements for the top and cut a straight piece the length of the circumference for the sides. Join with clear tape to form the fez shape (A).

2 Cover the shape, inside and out, with plastic wrap to make it waterproof (B).

3 Put the shape on a hat block or over an upturned bowl on the work surface, and cover with teased out strips of wool that cross over the top and cover the sides of the hat.

A

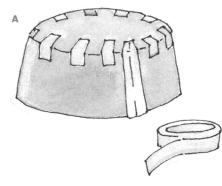

B

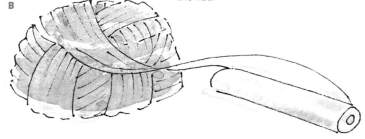

**4** Create a second layer perpendicular to the first layer.

**5** Cover the hat with a net, and sprinkle with warm, soapy water. Pat and press the fibers down onto the shape.

C

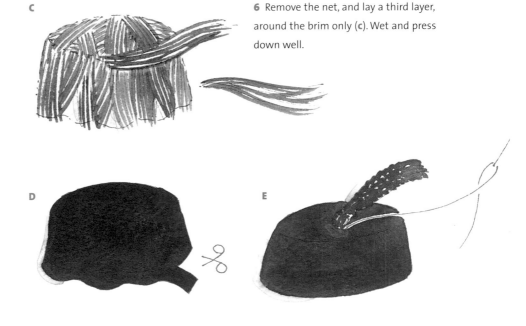

**6** Remove the net, and lay a third layer, around the brim only (**c**). Wet and press down well.

## felting the hat

**1** Sprinkle the hat with hot, soapy water and rub the fibers together well for 10 to 15 minutes. Test to see how well the fleeces have felted by removing it from the block. You may need to continue rubbing for a longer time.

**2** Once the hat is well felted, trim away the excess felt from the edge of the brim, using a pair of scissors (**D**).

D                    E

## finishing the hat

**1** Remove the hat from the block, squeeze out the excess water and rinse thoroughly. Put the damp hat back on the block to dry.

**2** Mold the hat into shape and make sure the brim is even.

**3** Decorate with a tassel or attach a line of braid around the join between the crown and the brim (**E**).

# small purse

This decorative little purse is very simply made using a plastic resist, so there are no side seams to stitch. The top layer of felt is decorated with a swirling design in two to three other colors, randomly scattered over the surface, but you could use any textured design if you prefer. The little spotted pattern on the slippers on page 86 would also look good on a small purse. The long strap is created by laying down the top for flat felt using a table edge as a guide. The funky button is made from a roll of multicolored layered felt (see page 45).

## MATERIALS

1½ OZ (50 G) MERINO WOOL
TOP FOR OUTSIDE; ¾ OZ
(20 G) MERINO WOOL TOP
FOR LINING

SMALL PIECES OF FLEECE

FELTING EQUIPMENT (SEE
PAGE 34), PLUS RESIST

SCISSORS

NEEDLE AND THREAD

# HOW TO MAKE IT

The sweet little purse could easily be enlarged to make a bigger, more daring bag, provided you increase the quantities of wool top. If you make the inner layer of felt from a contrasting color, it creates an attractive lining to the bag. Touches of inlaid colored wool in the top layer give it additional interest, and it is finished with a strap made by laying down the top for flat felt using a table edge as a guide. The purse shown here measures 6 by 4" (15 by 10 cm), so you will need a larger template to allow for shrinkage and the flap.

## creating the design

**1** Cut out a plastic resist to the shape required. Remember to add an extra 1" (2.5 cm) all around for shrinkage.

**2** Lay the resist on the prepared work

surface and tease out tufts in the lining color about 4" (10 cm) long and lay them side by side on the template (**A**), overlapping the edges of the template by about 1" (2.5 cm).

**3** Cover with the net and sprinkle with warm, soapy water. Press flat. Remove the net, turn the piece over, and fold the edges over plastic.

**4** Lay down another layer of tufts in the outside color (as in Step 2) on the other side of the plastic. Repeat Step 3.

**5** Create a second layer of outside color tufts as in Steps 2 and 3, with each layer

perpendicular to the previous layer.

**6** Add a third perpendicular layer on both sides, laying down small tufts of colors in the desired design (**B**).

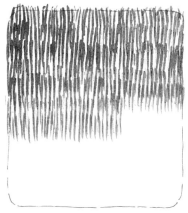

A

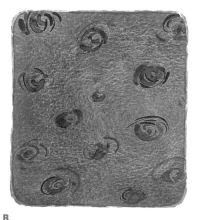

B

**7** Cover the finished shape with a net and sprinkle with warm water. Gently rub soap over the net. Taking care not to move the elements of the design, rub with both hands in a polishing movement for about 10 minutes. Turn the shape over and repeat the process on the other side of the resist.

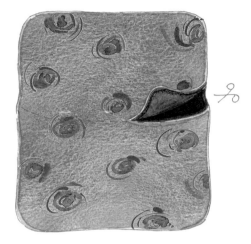

C

## creating the flap

**1** Once the purse is felted, mark a section on one side to leave a flap on the other side.

**2** Measure down the bag to the required point and, using sharp scissors, cut away the flap area (c). Set the excess fabric aside. Roll the purse in a blind or around a stick, pour very hot water over it, and roll it backward and forward for 10 minutes or until the felt hardens.

**3** Finish off the flap area by working it with your fingers, using a little soap, so that it is well rubbed in and firm. Cut a buttonhole in the center front.

## making the strap

**1** Make the strap from a single piece of flat felt. Lay out the fibers parallel with a table edge to ensure that it is straight. Lay tufts 3" (8 cm) long horizontally, lay down a second layer perpendicular to the first, and the last layer as the first. Felt (see pages 35–36), rinse, and allow to dry.

**2** Fold the felt in half lengthways (D) and stitch the long sides together using contrasting thread. Overcast each end to close, and stitch the strap securely to the bag at the two sides.

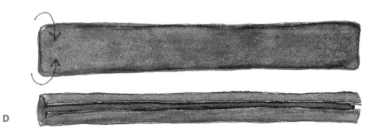

D

## finishing the purse

Make a button by cutting through the excess fabric to create a strip ¼" (1 cm) wide (see page 45). Roll it up into a circle. Using a darning needle and embroidery thread in a matching color, stab stitch through the center of the button to secure it. Stitch the button to the purse front.

**MATERIALS**

¾ OZ (20 G) MERINO WOOL
   TOP IN ONE COLOR
   (OUTSIDE)

¾ OZ (20 G) MERINO WOOL
   TOP IN SECOND COLOR
   (INSIDE)

FELTING EQUIPMENT (SEE
   PAGE 34)

PLASTIC RESIST

CONTRASTING EMBROIDERY
   THREAD AND NEEDLE

SCISSORS

SILK CORD AND SNAPS

# HOW TO MAKE A GLASSES CASE

This design could be adapted to make a purse just as easily (see pages 106–107). The delicate flower that decorates the flap has been outlined with embroidery. Its appeal lies in the simplicity of the design and in limiting the color palette to give it greater graphic impact. Use an existing glasses case for the pattern.

## creating the design

1 Cut out a pattern for the resist, with a couple more inches on the length to allow for the flap and allowing a little extra all around for shrinkage.

2 Put the template on the prepared work surface. Using the inside color, lay down the teased-out tufts side by side, facing the same direction, on the plastic resist, overlapping the edges by an inch or so.

3 Cover with a net curtain, sprinkle with warm, soapy water, and pat down the tufts. Once they are all in place, remove the net and turn the piece over. Turn over the excess tufts around the edges.

4 Repeat these steps on the other side of the resist, ensuring that the tufts of felt are laid down perpendicular to the first layer. Turn under the edges as before and repeat the process.

5 Using the outside color, repeat the same process for the second layer, laying down the tufts perpendicular to the previous layer.

6 Using the outside color again, create a third layer on both sides of the resist (A), following the steps as before, but ensuring that the wool top is perpendicular to the previous layer. Add a small quantity of tufts of the first color at one end of the case.

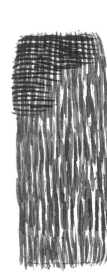

A

## felting the case

1 Cover the shape with the net. Sprinkle with hot water, rub the surface with soap, and then rub with both hands in a polishing action, and continue to rub for 10 minutes or so. Turn the shape over and repeat the process for 10 minutes on the other side. By now the shape will have started to pull on the plastic, as the fibers shrink down.

2 Once the felt has hardened, you can cut the flap. Remove one section from one end of the felt oval as shown (B), remove the plastic resist, and set this aside. Then cut out the piece of felt (it can be used for the flower decoration later).

3 Roll the piece up in the blind or wrap it around the stick and tie in place. Roll the stick or blind backward and forward until the felt has become firmer and the shape has shrunk down a little. Continue to roll backward and forward until it reaches the desired size. Full the seam areas further by hand to round them out.

4 Rinse the felted case and the excess felt in fresh water to remove the soap; allow to dry.

B

## finishing the case

1 Attach a cord to the sides of the case, on the inside, overcasting the ends securely. Stitch snaps to the inside of the flap and the matching point on the front of the case (C).

2 Make a small flower (see page 27). Cut a circle for the center and stitch it onto the flower and to the flap of the case. If you wish, you can embroider the center to create the stamens for a point of interest.

C

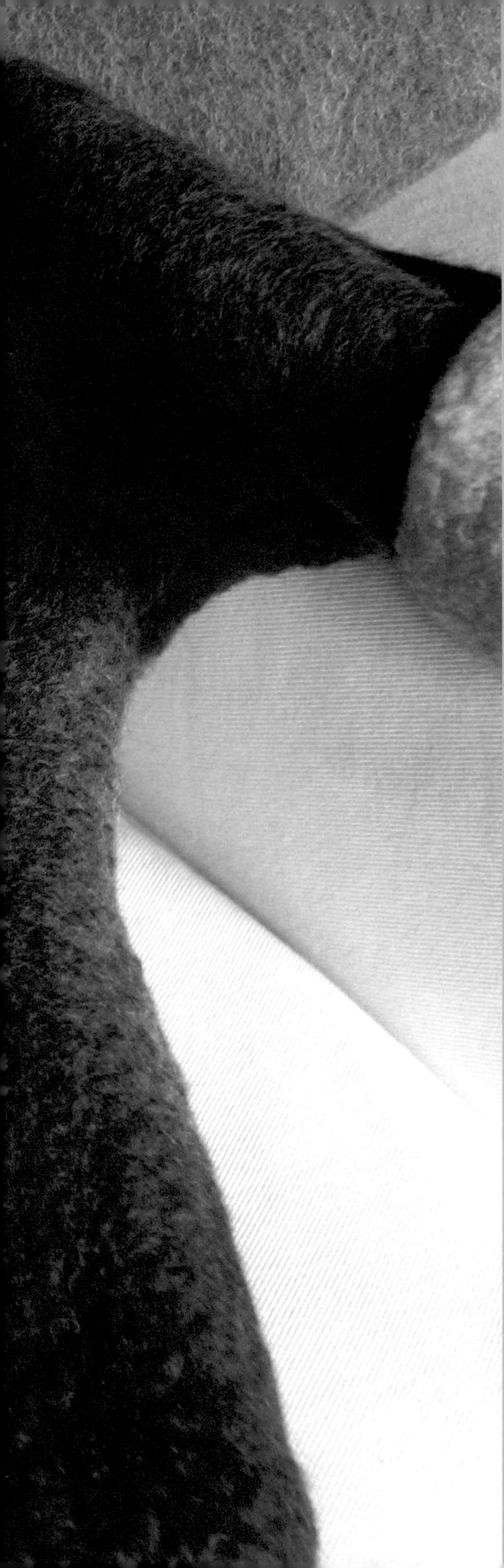

# child's silk-lined jacket

The jacket shown here would fit a six-year-old child (it has a 28" [70 cm] chest), but you can adapt the pattern to fit an adult. The charm of this jacket lies in the beautiful texture of its tussah silk lining and the delicate inlaid silk design on the front and back of the jacket. The jacket is fully reversible. You can make a completely plain one (one color on one side, one on the other) or a more decorated version, like this—as you wish.

**MATERIALS**

**9 oz (250 g) Merino wool top**

**1½ oz (50 g) tussah silk for the lining and decoration**

**Plastic resist**

**Felting equipment (see page 34)**

**Scissors**

# HOW TO MAKE IT

First of all decide on any pattern you might like to incorporate on one side of the jacket, and ensure that you have an adequate quantity of the tussah silk. Then take the measurements around the chest, the length from neck to hip, and wrist to neck for the sleeves, and cut a template for the plastic resist to these measurements (see page 124), allowing a little extra all around for shrinkage. If you are lining the jacket with silk or another color, this will be laid down first, directly on the resist. Any pattern or decoration on the outside layer will be the last to be laid down.

## creating the felt

**1** Prepare the work surface. On the plastic template, lay down strands of tussah silk for the lining. Tease out tufts of wool top into 5" (12 cm) lengths and lay down on top of the silk, side by side, all facing in the same direction, and continue until the resist is covered, allowing the wool top to overlap the edges.

**2** Cover with the net, sprinkle with warm, soapy water, and press flat with your hands.

**3** Turn over and fold the excess wool over the edges. Then lay down a layer of tussah silk and wool top on this side of the resist (repeating Steps 1 and 2).

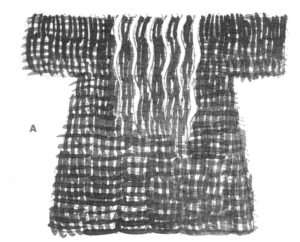

A

**4** Turn the resist over to the first side, and repeat the process with the wool top only (making sure that the fibers in each layer are perpendicular to those underneath).

**5** Repeat the process again to create a third layer of wool top, laid perpendicular to those underneath. Finally, incorporate any chosen pattern of tussah silk (**A**) for decoration.

# the felting process

1 Follow the felting steps (see pages 35–36), rubbing for about 15 minutes on the first side, and 15 minutes on the second side. By now the wool will have started to shrink and will be pulling on the plastic shape. Rub for a little longer, paying particular attention to the arms, the bottom edge of the jacket, and the neckline, to ensure that they have felted evenly. (It is easy in felting to neglect these areas, leading to weak, soft felt at these points.) Make sure the decoration has bonded to the wool top (try to lift the silk fibers to check) and continue rubbing for a little longer if necessary.

B

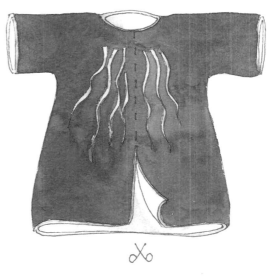

2 With a sharp pair of scissors, cut along the bottom of the jacket and remove the resist. Draw a line down the mid-center point of the front of the jacket, and cut down this line to create the jacket opening (B).

3 Cut the sleeve openings and trim the front neck a little to create a gentle curve.

4 Remove the plastic resist.

# finishing the jacket

1 To harden the felt, roll the jacket in a rattan blind, pour very hot water over it, and roll backward and forward, in each direction, for 3–4 minutes or until it is hard.

2 Rinse out the soap carefully and hang to dry.

3 To ensure a good rounded shape, put your hand into the sleeves and full them futher by hand. Work the seam areas further by hand to round them off.

**ALTERNATIVE MOTIF**
A spiral pattern, shown here created in pale blue wool top and white tussah silk, makes an attractive alternative design. You could easily adapt the jacket design to make a small pinafore dress in the same way, using this design for the front.

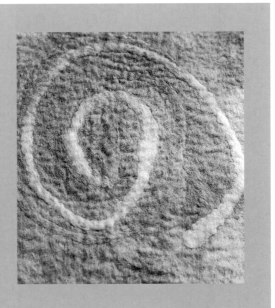

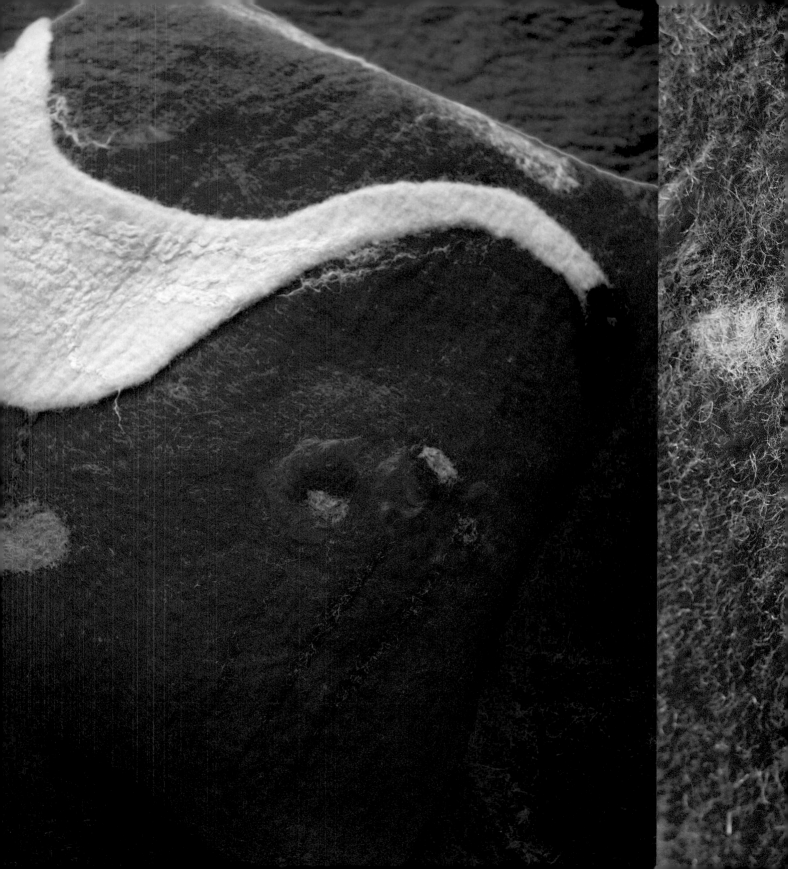

# pictorial pillow

Felt makes a good background fabric for embroidery. This pillow cover is more decorative than many of the projects in this book, and is ideal for those who enjoy surface detail. The goose is made up from pieces of soft (pre-felted) felt—in other words felt that has not been hardened. Threads and silk have also been employed in the design. The cover is made without side seams, using a plastic resist (see pages 80–81).

**MATERIALS**

3 OZ (90 G) MERINO WOOL
    TOP FOR THE PILLOW
    AND THE GOOSE

SMALL QUANTITY OF WOOL
    TOP AND TUSSAH SILK
    FOR DECORATION

PLASTIC RESIST

FELTING EQUIPMENT (SEE
    PAGE 34)

WOOL YARN

PILLOW FORM

# HOW TO MAKE IT

You will need to make a piece of two-layered felt around a square resist to the measurements of your pillow (see pages 80–81). This one measures 12 by 12" (30 by 30 cm). You will also need small scraps of soft felt in appropriate colors for the body of the goose, its beak, legs, feet, and the flowers with stems. The patches of color in the sky are created from inlaid silk fibers. These are then rubbed into the last layer of the felt (as on page 68). You can copy this design or revise it according to the felt colors you already have. A series of pillows with different animals would be fun! As another alternative, a fantastical bird in a different colorway with embroidered decoration is shown on the opposite page.

## creating the design

**1** You will need to follow the instructions on pages 80–81 for creating a felt shape using a plastic resist. In this case, the plastic resist is cut to the size of the finished pillow plus an inch (2.5 cm) all around for shrinkage. A second piece is needed for the body of the goose.

**2** Create the felt, laying down three layers of wool top on each side of the resist. The pieces are then felted (see page 35) but not fulled, so that the felt is still soft.

A

**3** Cut out the body shape for the goose, and cut the beak, legs, and feet from a small colored piece of left-over felt, and lay them down on the top of the pillow.

**4** Add the silk threads for the sky and clouds, and some yarns and threads for the flowers (A).

# the felting process

**1** Cover with a net and, using olive oil soap, rub the pillow (see page 35), taking care not to disturb the surface design; rub until these additional areas bond with the surface of the pillow. Then carry out the fulling process (see page 36).

**2** When the pillow has shrunk, you can make a cut in the center back on the reverse of the pillow, and remove the plastic resist.

# finishing the pillow

**1** Punch two holes in each side of the opening on the back of the cushion and thread a length of brightly colored yarn through the holes (**B**).

**2** Insert the pillow form and tie the yarn in a little bow (**C**).

**B**

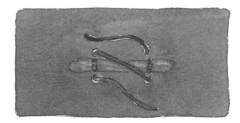

**C**

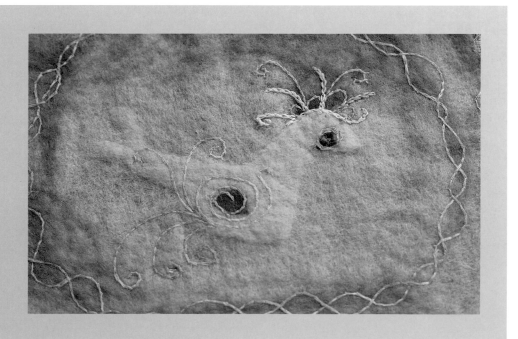

**ALTERNATIVE MOTIF**

This little bird is made in much the same way as the goose—with an inlaid piece of felt rubbed in—but some additional surface decoration in the form of embroidery is added afterwards. You can use embroidery successfully to highlight areas of a design.

# useful information

In the following pages, we offer advice on dealing with raw wool, the care of finished felt, dyeing fiber with natural dyes, troubleshooting, and making little flowers to add to the projects, as well as some basic information on cutting and stitching. Here, you'll also find project templates and a Suppliers section that includes addresses and websites for felting materials suppliers, and felting organizations and societies.

# PREPARING FLEECES

Although the instructions in this book use scoured, combed wool top, you may have occasion to prepare your own. If you do, be aware that the quality of fleeces varies, as does their suitability for felting. The nature of the fleece depends on the breed of sheep, whose wool has different qualities. Indeed, within one fleece sheared from a sheep, there will be variations, depending on whether it has come from the back, underbelly, or legs of the sheep (exposure to weather, for example, varies the thickness). Merino sheep have particularly fine wool, which felts easily, but there are other coarser fleeces available, for example Finn or Karakul sheep fleeces, which are ideal for rugs or other hard-wearing projects.

## WASHING THE FLEECE

Put on rubber gloves and wear protective clothing. Fill a large plastic bucket, three quarters full with hand-hot water and add a drop or two of wool-safe soap such as Dawn dishwashing soap or Eucalan, to the water. Place 8 oz (250 g) of wool into a mesh bag and slowly lower it into the bucket and let it soak for 15 minutes. Do not be tempted to prod the fleece—leave it undisturbed. After 15 minutes, gently lift the fiber out of the water and squeeze out the excess water. Gently lower the fiber into another bucket filled with water at the same temperature as the dirty water. Continue to rinse in this way until the water is clear. Do not run water directly over the wool as it can cause premature felting. Squeeze out the excess water and use the spin cycle on the washer to extract any extra water. Make sure to remove the fiber before the wash cycle continues. Lay the fiber on a towel to dry.

## CARDING

Prepare the fibers for felting by carding with handcards or a drumcarder. Handcards and drumcarders are used to open up the fibers and organize them. The fine teeth held in the carding cloth on both these tools are created to gently comb the fibers without breaking them. For detailed instructions on preparing your wool for felting, see Lee Raven's books, *Hands on Spinning*, and *Spin It!* (Interweave Press, 1987 and 2003).

# DYEING WOOL

Although you can buy dyed wool in many wonderful colors, it is useful, too, to be able to dye your own wool on occasion. You can use either natural or synthetic dyes. Experiments with color are always exciting, and using ingredients for color from the natural world gives a particular thrill. There are some excellent books on natural dyes, including Rita Buchanan's *A Dyer's Garden* (Interweave Press, 1995), and Dagmar Klos's *The Dyer's Companion* (Interweave Press, 2004). There are many different dyes and methods of dyeing that can be used. The subject is well worth studying in greater depth if you continue to do a lot of felting, but for now, here are a couple of easy vegetable dyeing methods. The results are very beautiful and the process uncomplicated!

Though dyeing with natural dyes is less toxic than synthetic dyes, it is best to take some precautions. Dye in a well-ventilated space; Wear a dust mask when working with powders; Don't use kitchen utensils or pots—have a set of dye equipment that is just for dyeing; Dispose of mordant baths down the sink and flush with a lot of water.

In the standard dyeing process, the fiber absorbs the color in the dyebath. The color is fixed to the fiber with a mordant (normally alum).

### ONION SKINS

Onion skins make one of the best known natural dyes. They produce a range of delicate colors from orange-gold to buttery yellow to cream, depending on how strong the dyebath is. The recipe below is for 4 oz (100 g) of scoured wool. You will need a small quantity of alum and cream of tartar for the mordant.

4 oz (124 g) scoured fleece or wool top
1 oz (30 g) onion skins

¼ oz (7 g) alum (mordant)
¼ oz (7 g) cream of tartar

### MORDANT BATH

Wearing a dust mask, dissolve the alum and cream of tartar in a little hot water and add a large pan three quarters full of water. Wet the fleece and add to the mordant bath. Slowly raise the temperature and gently simmer for 45 minutes. Watch the pot carefully, but don't stir the wool as it will felt easily. Take off the heat and allow the bath to cool. Remove the fiber, squeeze out the excess moisture, and gently rinse by lowering into a bucket of rinse water at the same temperature as the dyebath.

### DYEBATH

Place the onion skins in a large pan three quarters full of water. Bring to a boil, and then simmer for about 45 minutes. Remove from heat, retrieve the onion skins, and allow to cool.

When the dyebath has cooled, add enough water to allow free movement of the fiber. Put in the well-wetted fleece. Bring the dyebath to a gentle simmer, and allow to simmer for 40 minutes or until the color has reached the shade desired. Take the fleece from the dyebath, allow it to cool and then rinse as above in several changes of water (at the same temperature). Lay on a towel to dry.

### COCHINEAL DYE

Cochineal produces some wonderfully soft and rich russet and pink shades. The cochineal is actually a tiny beetle.

1 oz (25 g) cochineal (whole)
¼ tsp lemon juice
4 oz (124 g) scoured fleece or wool top

Pour boiling water on the cochineal and simmer gently for 30–45 minutes. Strain the dye liquid and leave to cool before use.

Add a quarter of a teaspoon of lemon juice and stir well. At this point, the color of the dye bath will change from purple to red. Be sparing with the quantity of lemon juice as using too much will turn the dyebath orange. When you have the shade you want, add 8 oz (250 g) of wetted out wool. Bring the pot gradually to a gentle simmer and simmer for 30–45 minutes. Leave to cool, and then rinse as for the onion skins until the rinse water is clear. Lay on a towel to dry.

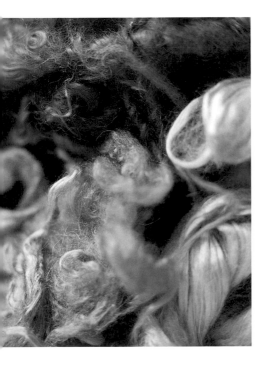

**Above:** The colors resulting from dyeing tussah silk using onion skin and cochineal on dyes.

**Right:** The colors resulting from dyeing Merino wool top in different strengths of the same dyes.

# STITCHING

Some of the projects require simple stitching to create the final effect. For thick felt, you may need a special curved felting needle, but for most projects a normal large-eyed embroidery or darning needle will suffice. Mark any stitching line in tailor's chalk first to ensure it is straight. You can embroider on thinner pieces of felt, and many projects require simple seaming. The basic stitch used in these pages is stab stitch (a version of running stitch well suited for going through layers of felt). More decorative stitches include chain stitches and French knots. Some projects require basting before stitching. Basting is simply an elongated form of running stitch. Other projects call for overcasting, which is similar to stab stitching, but worked closely together.

### backstitch

Backstitching creates a line of stitches with no space between them; it looks like a drawn line. The stitches are worked so that the needle is taken back to the finishing point of the first stitch, to create what appears to be a continuous line.

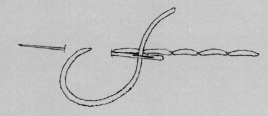

### stab stitch

The stab stitch resembles running stitch and is used to stitch together layers of fabric in a simple seam. The needle and thread are taken first up and then down through the layers of fabric to produce neat straight stitches at evenly spaced intervals.

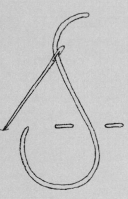

### chain stitch

Chain stitches are worked in a line, the thread forming a loop on the surface of the fabric. It is used for decorative purposes. To create the stitch, bring the needle up through the fabric, loop the thread around the needle, take the needle down and then bring it up again just within the loop to create a row of chains.

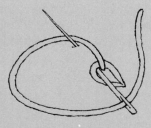

### French knot

These decorative stitches form small individual knots. To work the stitch, bring the needle and thread up through the fabric, twist the thread around the needle a couple of times and then take the needle back through the fabric in the same place, holding the loop with the thumb while you do so. Pull tight.

# FELT FLOWERS

These very simple decorative flowers can be used to adorn hats, book covers, bags or whatever felted projects you fancy. You can vary the size, shape, and complexity to suit the style of your project. You can also string them together, if you wish, to make a necklace!

### simple flower shapes

Cut two circles from contrasting colored pieces of felt, one slightly smaller than the other (use a circular template such as a coin or the base of a small glass). Stab stitch together.

### multipetaled flowers

You can make a flower with a more floppy appearance, either as a single or a double flower. If you use two colors with a contrasting color on one side of the felt, it will look more ornate.

### flower buds

To make a flower bud shape, cut out two circles and then cut through the center of each, so that you have four semi-circles. Stitch these together end-to-end, overlapping slightly, and then roll the length of semicircles up into a bud shape, fanning the outer edges. Textured felt with silky fibers added to it produces a lovely sheen.

### necklace of flowers

From two thin layers of flat felt, cut out a number of small circles, about an inch in diameter. Fold them in half, and then in half again. Take a piece of silver jewelry wire and push it through the base of each folded piece of felt. Space the shapes out as you wish along the wire, and twist the wire behind each shape so that it does not move. Cut the wire to the required length and add a jewelry fastening. If you want a softer look, thread the flowers onto thread.

# TEMPLATES

The reproduction size for each template varies so photocopy to the required size for the project. Use a lightbox (a piece of glass on a box frame with a lightbulb under it makes a good home-made version) to trace off the design onto a piece of cardboard or paper, which can then be used for the pattern for seamed pieces or use it to make a resist for seamless ones.

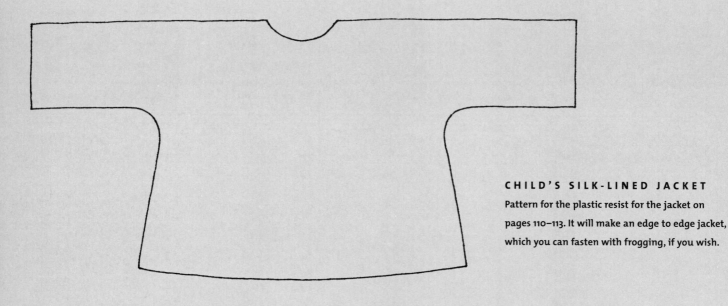

### CHILD'S SILK-LINED JACKET
Pattern for the plastic resist for the jacket on pages 110–113. It will make an edge to edge jacket, which you can fasten with frogging, if you wish.

### SLIPPERS AND BOOTIES
This basic template serves for both slippers and booties on page 87. Enlarge as required for appropriate sizing. Simply cut away the ankle and upper areas after felting to the shape required.

For the children's booties on page 87, cut the toe portion into a more pointed shape and enlarge as needed.

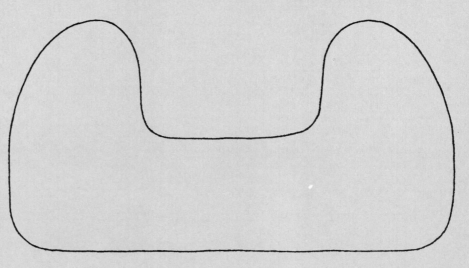

**BUCKET BAG**

The basic shape for the bucket bag on pages
74–77. The triangular gussets are inverted
when making up the bag, so that the
pointed end is at the base.

**CLOCHE HAT**

This is the bell-shaped pattern for the hat
on pages 98–101. Measure the
circumference of your head, and enlarge
the template to the required size (half of
the circumference, plus one third).

# CARE OF FELT

Once you have created your felt projects, you will need to look after them and keep them clean. You can wash the felt if you do so carefully. Put the piece into a basin or bowl of lukewarm water to which a proprietary liquid wool soap has already been added. Push the felt around until enough of the liquid has been thoroughly absorbed. Very gently, squeeze it to remove any dirt.

Rinse the felt well in cool, clear water, and do so several times until the water runs clear and all traces of soap have been removed.

Use the spin cycle on the washing machine to spin out the excess water, but remove it before the wash cycle begins. Gently pull the piece of felt back to its original shape. Dry on a line or on a rack. It can be pressed, if necessary, with a warm iron (protected with a cloth) or gently steamed.

Although some felt pieces could be washed in a washing machine on a cool wash, you do run the risk of shrinkage, so take care.

Dry cleaning is also possible for felt made from commercial-dyed wool top.

## TROUBLESHOOTING

Just in case you are experiencing problems with felt making, here are some common problems and their solutions.

### • Laying down layers unevenly
Take time to ensure the tufts of wool top are laid down in similar quantities, and very evenly. Uneven layers will lead to uneven felt.

### • Edges
Many people fail to ensure that the edges of the felt, particularly when working with a resist, are thick enough. Ensure the wool tops are laid down evenly and that you pay attention to edges when rubbing and felting.

### • Rubbing in
When rubbing in your design, be it loose fibers or a cut-out inlay, take care not to move it around too much. Rub the design in first, before rubbing in the whole area.

To ease rubbing, smooth soap over the net. It will make rubbing easier and is kinder on your hands. You may want to use gloves to prevent your hands from chafing (a plastic bag over your hands will do just as well!).

When fulling the felt made with a resist, make sure you work into the seam areas by hand after rolling, to achieve an even, rounded shape.

### • Soap
Too much soap will make your piece slippery and difficult to work. If this happens, roll up the piece, squeeze out the excess soapy water and start again.

### • Water
Too much can slow felting down and make it hard to felt. You will learn to get the quantities just right the more you felt.

### • Water temperatures
After the initial felting, make sure you use very hot water to speed up the hardening and rolling process.

If bonding others fibers together, start with cool water and then use really hot water at the end.

### • Resists
When working with resists, make sure both sides are covered completely and evenly for strength. Ovelapping the edges with fibers will help to ensure this happens.